Body Image and Eating Disorders

One of the paradoxes of our current era is that only 10 percent of obese or overweight people are actually dieting, whereas nearly 20 percent of the remaining population are trying to lose weight, even if they do not need to. This volume looks into our contemporary relationship with food by inserting current body image and eating disorders, like orthorexia and bigorexia, into a broader historical overview. Fabio Gabrielli and Floriana Irtelli combine their knowledge of psychoanalysis and anthropology with scientific research and clinical experience to create this truly interdisciplinary work. Their study uses psychoanalytical theories about our "hypermodern" times to trace the impact that mass media has on individuals, families, and societies. It explores various "food tribes" and exposes the contradictions of today's mass media that advertise fitness and dieting alongside increasingly tasty and accessible foods. The work helps us understand our highly social relationship with our bodies and what we eat.

FABIO GABRIELLI has been Professor of Philosophical Anthropology and Dean of the Faculty of Human Sciences at Ludes University of Lugano, Switzerland. He currently teaches philosophy of relationship at the School of Management of LUM-Jean Monnet University (Milan campus). He is also a visiting professor at PWSTE-University of Jaroslaw, Poland. He has been working for many years on philosophy applied to medicine, with particular reference to the relationship between doctor and patient. He is author of several essays and scientific articles.

FLORIANA IRTELLI is a lecturer at the Catholic University of the Sacred Heart, Milan. She is a psychoanalyst and psychotherapist. Irtelli also works at the Fatebenefratelli Hospital, Milan, performing research and clinical activities. She has edited collections, including *Psychosis: Biopsychosocial and Relational Perspectives* (2018) and *Family Therapy* (2019). Her most recent book is *Contemporary Perspectives on Relational Wellness: Psychoanalysis and the Modern Family* (2018).

T0370561

Body Image and Eating Disorders

An Anthropological and Psychological Overview

FABIO GABRIELLI
Ludes University, Lugano

FLORIANA IRTELLI
Catholic University of the Sacred Heart, Milan

CAMBRIDGE
UNIVERSITY PRESS

CAMBRIDGE
UNIVERSITY PRESS

University Printing House, Cambridge CB2 8BS, United Kingdom

One Liberty Plaza, 20th Floor, New York, NY 10006, USA

477 Williamstown Road, Port Melbourne, VIC 3207, Australia

314–321, 3rd Floor, Plot 3, Splendor Forum, Jasola District Centre,
New Delhi – 110025, India

103 Penang Road, #05–06/07, Visioncrest Commercial, Singapore 238467

Cambridge University Press is part of the University of Cambridge.

It furthers the University's mission by disseminating knowledge in the pursuit of
education, learning, and research at the highest international levels of excellence.

www.cambridge.org
Information on this title: www.cambridge.org/9781316514306
DOI: 10.1017/9781009082983

First published 2022

A catalogue record for this publication is available from the British Library.

Library of Congress Cataloging-in-Publication Data
Names: Gabrielli, Fabio (Clinical practitioner), author. | Irtelli, Floriana, author.
Title: Body image and eating disorders : an anthropological and psychological
overview / Fabio Gabrielli, Ludes University, Floriana Irtelli, Catholic University
of the Sacred Heart.
Description: Cambridge, United Kingdom ; New York, NY : Cambridge University
Press, 2022. | Includes index.
Identifiers: LCCN 2021057928 (print) | LCCN 2021057929 (ebook) | ISBN
9781316514306 (hardback) | ISBN 9781009078030 (paperback) | ISBN
9781009082983 (ebook)
Subjects: LCSH: Body image – Psychological aspects. | Eating disorders –
Psychological aspects. | BISAC: PSYCHOLOGY / Applied Psychology
Classification: LCC BF697.5.B63 G33 2022 (print) | LCC BF697.5.B63 (ebook) |
DDC 306.4/613–dc23/eng/20211217
LC record available at https://lccn.loc.gov/2021057928
LC ebook record available at https://lccn.loc.gov/2021057929

ISBN 978-1-316-51430-6 Hardback
ISBN 978-1-009-07803-0 Paperback

Contents

Acknowledgments

Thanks to Dr. Benedetta Pedraglio for the linguistic suggestions and the drafting of the index, and thanks to Dr. Emanuele Proverbio for the fundamental IT support and technical support.

PART I Contemporary Perspectives in Anthropology, Philosophy, and Psychology on the Human Body: An Introductory Overview

1 The Conception of the Human Body: An Evolutionary Study from Ancient Times to the Hypermodern Era

1.1 THE HYPERMODERN CONCEPT OF THE BODY: ANTHROPOLOGICAL IMPLICATIONS

One should accept one's body as one's home, a living space designated for communication and relationships. We live in a highly complex time deeply marked by the digital revolution, an infosphere that has produced radical transformations (Louw, 2017), increasingly conspicuous acquisitions of cognitive neuroscience, and all related anthropological fallouts.[1] Our time witnesses the hybridization of humans and machines, confronting us with the onerous problem of new forms and the effective consistency of post-human freedom. The body is now in danger of changing structurally into a thing:[2] the merging of the human body with machines entails certain potentially burdensome problems pertaining to the concept of a "post-human" freedom wherein the body is probably transforming anatomically into something new.[3]

---

[1] The infosphere is an environment populated by informational entities. For further details, see Perucchietti (2019), Floridi (2017), Carbone (2016), Prensky (2013), Carr (2011), and Grion (2012).

[2] For a critical review of cognitive neuroscience, see Ehrenberg (2019).

[3] "Having exhausted the great historical task of confronting God and the animal, which has lasted in the West since the time of the ancient Greeks, it is now the thing that demands all our attention and raises the most pressing question: it has become both the center of upheaval and the promise of happiness" (Perniola, 1994, p. 18). Again, "If we look for something in common experiences that presents analogies with the neutral feeling of [alienation from oneself], we find it in drug addictions and in particular those caused by opium and its derivatives ... The general tone of the junkie seems to be characterized by feeling his body as a thing, by becoming a foreign body as much as a garment, by escaping the cycle of tension, discharge and rest" (Perniola, 1994, p. 18). All translations from foreign language texts are the authors' own unless otherwise stated. For an effective critical summary of these topics, see Scardovi (2017).

How has the topic of the body been treated in previous ages? Evidently, the perspective of human physicality has changed over time.

> In many philosophies of life and religious circles, as influenced by Platonic dualism (the body is merely an inferior prison of the human soul), there is immediately the association that the human body, with its sensual needs, is from a lower order and should be suppressed in a Stoic way ...
>
> Scepticism regarding the value of the sensual human body with its passions and sexual needs can be traced back to what one can call the *Platonic dualism in anthropology*. For example, Plato provides us with the idea that a soul can be deprived of its body; that it does not come fully into its own until it has been separated from the body, and that it is immortal. The body is therefore merely clothing for the soul, a kind of prison from which it should escape and be liberated.
>
> In general, the human body was in many religious circles and philosophies of life excluded from "soulfulness" and reduced to the realm of "flesh."
>
> (Louw, 2017, p. 42)

The body represents a significant theme that has induced innumerable reflections since the beginning of human civilization. The relationship between body and mind has conceptually affected human beings since ancient times. Alternative positions have been taken over the centuries, either supporting a separation between the *soma* (Greek, "body") and the psyche (Greek *psychē* meaning "breath, principle of life, life, soul") or endorsing the existence of psychosomatic unity. As may be anticipated, Plato was the first supporter of the dualist theory (i.e., the separation between mind and body). He introduced the distinction between the soul and the body as substances that are independent of each other and that are irreducible. The soul was considered immortal and conceived as the seat of higher consciousness and mental functions that continued to exist after the death of the body. Conversely, the body without life (i.e., after death) was cognized as becoming an object. The Platonic vision was resumed and accentuated by Descartes almost 2,000 years later. He deemed the mind and the body to be completely separate entities, considering the mind to represent the phenomenon within which all human knowledge was vested. Descartes theorized that the mind could not be positioned at the same level as material reality; therefore, the body was a machine governed by the mind.

The holistic vision opposes the dualist view, postulating a unity between mind and body. The origins of this conception can be traced with certainty to the earliest historically documented periods of human civilization. The first definitive studies on the psychosomatic unity of the human body and mind are dated to the time of the Hippocratic school. Aristotle also recognized this psychosomatic unity, claiming that the soul shaped the body; thus, the soul could not be separated from its material form (see Frati, 2012).

Common psychological phenomena, such as a slight feeling of joy or fear, affect the body; on the other hand, particularly stressful emotional tensions occurring in succession can cause organ diseases such as gastric ulcers. The psychosomatic approach is, therefore, an attempt to see people in their entirety. It is based on the key concept that a person represents an inseparable biological unity comprising both body and mind. An individual is constructed not only of a biological body but also of psychic and emotional factors that dis-charge decisive roles in a person's balance and in the genesis and development of diseases.[4] Recently, the body has been regarded as the primary vessel through which we can open up to the world (Galimberti, 1983; Frati, 2012), and this notion is widely exemplified in the philosophical ideas of Friedrich Wilhelm Nietzsche and Maurice Merleau-Ponty.[5] The body's significance was subsequently

[4]   For an overview of the body in Western thought, see Galimberti's (1983) dated but still useful essay, *Il corpo*, and Frati (2012).
[5]   See Nietzsche (1964, p. 34): "Wherever the doctrine of pure spirituality was dominant, it destroyed nervous energy with its aberrations: it taught to hold the body in contempt, to neglect or torment it, and to torment and despise man himself, because of all his

emphasized by biopolitics (an intersectional discipline straddling human biology and politics) and biopower (the research domain related to the practices of modern nation-states and the regulation of their subjects through an explosion of numerous techniques aimed at the subjugation of bodies and the control of populations).[6] Gilles Deleuze's exposition of the mechanisms of "modern societies of control" underlined the body's significance.[7] Such concepts have highlighted the importance of the body and illuminated how some dogmas presume the soma.

The central role taken on by the body is still evident, as can be observed on several fronts:

- Although cognitive neurosciences have made extraordinary discoveries, they pose the risk of conceiving of and perceiving human beings only as neuronal entities and not as social beings. On the contrary, Alain Ehrenberg iterates that we must always remember the importance of social aspects and the whole body, not just the neuronal element. According to Ehrenberg (2019), it is therefore impossible to describe the role occupied by cognitive neurosciences, the meanings they have for us,

---

instincts; it created darkened souls, charged with tension and oppressed, who, moreover, believed they knew the cause of their sense of abjection and could perhaps eliminate it – it must reside in the body! This is always still too flourishing! – so they concluded, when in reality the body, with its pains, elevates protests upon protests against the continuous irritation." However, the body is very important because it is the main vessel through which we encounter the world: "If it is true that I am aware of my body through the world . . . for the same reason, my body is the pivot of the world, and in this sense I am aware of the world through my body" (Merleau-Ponty, 1972, p. 130).

6 Foucault wrote about biopolitics and biopower. He noted that the body has been conceptualized as a machine, from the strengthening of its attitudes, the extortion of its forces, and the parallel growth of its utility and docility to its integration with effective and economic control systems. It has been ensured by power mechanisms that characterize the anatomo-politics of the human body (for further details, see Foucault, 2004). The "enhancement of attitudes" asserted by Foucault with reference to the development of technologies in the seventeenth and eighteenth centuries does not seem too far from the "human enhancement" conceived by current advances in bioengineering. For an overview, see Campa (2015a, pp. 83–93) and Campa (2015b, pp. 125–170).

7 See Deleuze (2000). See also Velotti (2017) and Wolfe (2014) for further useful critical comparisons with the Deleuzian concept of "societies of control."

the uses we make of them, but also the concrete effects that the therapeutic methods that refer to them have on the individual, without also examining the different ways in which all these aspects are mixed with the rest of existence. Where the psychologist, the neuroscientist, or the sociologist try to reduce the human being to behaviors, he discovers that everything in him is intertwined.

- The hypermodern techniques of "human enhancement" are associated with an important ethical debate[8] that also allows reflection on the true signification of the term and its artificial implications.[9] From this perspective, the classic themes of human identity and human existence are now widely questioned in light of contemporary transformations (also on the human body) induced by technology, biology, and medicine. These themes lead to urgent contemplations:

> Reflecting on identity means, in fact, on the one hand, asking about oneself, opening up the question about the ego that remains the irreplaceable expression of one's lived individuality, as such irreducible to any other experience; on the other hand, it implies the awareness that this "self" is the original place where the very meaning of the human being, of that human condition, brings us back to the question about our nature, that is, about what was given to us in our coming into the world.
>
> *(Pessina, 2015, p. 450)*

- Current theories also posit the pragmatics of the body (as conceived by Deleuze), according to which the body is envisaged as a privileged setting for the employment of techniques and products aimed at unceasingly improving it and fully adhering to social recognition and other people's expectations.[10] This perspective illuminates the contemporary logic and

---

[8]   Savulescu and Bostrom (2008, p. 1) maintain that "In the past decade, human empowerment has become the major theme of the debate in applied ethics." Robotics and nanotechnologies are increasingly pushing the envelope. On the one hand, they are generating enthusiasm: the futurist Ray Kurzweil predicts that by 2045, "human intelligence will be improved a billion-fold thanks to high-tech brain extensions" (Wolfe, 2014); on the other hand, they cause serious concerns (see Longo, 2003).

[9]   This point is aptly elucidated by Palazzani (2015).

[10]   As mentioned previously, "the question of so-called *human enhancement* is articulated at two levels: first, a theoretical one, which sets up a debate that calls into question not only whether normativity exists in human nature but also whether it

dialectic of seduction.[11] In fact, this viewpoint pertains to all aspects of human life, from romantic relationships to the political world and from the cultural domain to the manufacturing of goods. It emerges from the processes of a new capitalism, not the consumerist vision of the past but a particularly seductive notion: Lipovetsky (2019) wrote that the seduction principle imposes itself as an omnipresent and trans-sectorial logic, since it is able to reorganize the power of the dominant spheres of social life and to reorganize ways of living from top to bottom, as well as the ways of coexistence of individuals. Liberal hypermodernity is inseparable from the generalization and supremacy of both the ethos and the mechanisms of seduction.

The current "society of seduction" exercises absolute control over the contemporary concept of the body and encourages a dizzying aesthetic market, particularly for women. It elevates technological beauty to a sort of desirable metaphysical utopic status (without limits, without imperfections, without vices, and even without death) (see Lipovetsky, 2019).

For example, in contemporary society, the female body tends to become an object of lust and seduction. In the social media, the female body was highjacked by business, companies, the

even makes sense to use this category, on the basis of evolutionary premises with the characteristics of true meta-physics. The other level, pragmatic in nature, which is in some ways winning, consists in enlarging the market of products that western citizens can resort to, in the hope of improving their own abilities to live up to social expectations and to their personal desires for self-fulfillment" (Pessina, 2015, p. 451).

[11]   We may recall Jean Baudrillard's (2002) definition: *universe of seduction* means what stands in radical opposition to the *universe of production*. It is not a matter of creating things, of producing them for a world of value, but a matter of seducing, meaning that we are diverting them from their value, their identity, their reality, to transform them according to the game of appearances (and seduction) – this is a symbolic exchange. A synthetic and incisive interpretation of Baudrillard's seduction may offer an interpretive key to post-humanism. (For further details, see Amendola, Del Gaudio, and Tirino, 2017; Lipovetsky, 2019, p. 14.) In this context, we are now more than ever witnessing a massive aesthetic visualization, with a marked female presence in symbolic codes and in imaginative social plots, in the name of extreme seduction: paradoxically, we see simultaneously the strong presence, the positivity and meaningful power of women, but also the great poverty of the social imaginary in which the production of fetish femininity is intensified, and where women are the objects of manipulation, remodeling, and restructuring. (For further details, see Braidotti, 2017.)

advertisement enterprise and the social media to sell products. The commodification of the female body contributes to the fact that femininity is constantly being robbed of soulful beauty and portrayed as an idol of glamour, fame and flirting sensuality.

(Louw, 2017, p. 53)

The aforementioned perspective evokes the following questions: how does present-day society perceive the human body? Which problems characterize current anthropological scenarios? We can also ask the following:

If one transfers the notion of beauty to human life, very specifically the naked human body, what would be the implication for theory formation in anthropology and the human quest for meaning and significance? Thus, the aesthetic question: For what purpose is the human body designed?

(Louw, 2017, p. 42)

I.2 MIGUEL BENASAYAG'S CONCEPTS OF FUNCTIONING AND EXISTENCE

The adjectives "modern," "postmodern," and "hypermodern" are labels that justify the innate human tendency to classify historical eras in addition to actual cultural epochal interruptions.[12]

According to Miguel Benasayag (2019), we use the term "hypermodern" to designate only the most advanced phase of the present-day crisis of reason. He believes that the current time represents a very irrational phase. The process of the crisis of reason began in the modern age with the decline of the Cartesian

---

[12] For an overview, see Franzini (2018). With respect to the undue simplification of the *modern* as a triumph of strong, founding, totalizing reason, and of the *postmodern* as praise for weak reason, of fragmentation, of multiplicity, Franzini shows the merit of highlighting the "liquid" traits of modernity, its moments of crisis, and its ideological plurality, which, in this sense, is common to the "postmodern." Some people prefer the term "neo-modernity." For further details, see Mordacci (2017).

philosophical concepts of clarity and distinction that typified rationalism and the recovery of ancient traditions in tandem with the myth of Vico (which does not obey merely objective Cartesian logic). Later, the Age of Enlightenment focused on reason but also recovered the aesthetic dimension through its progressive evolution of the Cartesian paradigm based on works by personalities such as Diderot, D'Alambert, and Bayle. The next historical period may be characterized by the dialectical consciousness of Hegel and continued into posterity through the concept of crisis theorized by Baudelaire, Benjamin, and Simmel. In our opinion, the crisis of reason typical of the contemporary hypermodern era can be explained through the set of theoretical concepts proposed by Benasayag: to function and to exist. Benasayag stated that there is currently no ontological fracture between these two dimensions; rather, there is some sort of hybridization:

> I want to make it clear right now that there is no "ontological" separation between these two dimensions: I do not mean to say that the functioning would be on the side of immediacy, of adaptive response and physical-chemical mechanisms, while existence would fall into the category of the superior principle, of some "vital force," or of a mystery of life.
>
> (Benasayag, 2019, p. 10)

In sum, human beings are now often metaphorically compared with machines that have to be efficient. Human existence is deemed similar to a functioning mechanism. Thus, there is a hybridization of the concepts of functioning and existing. However, human beings cannot be considered machines, and the contemporary crisis of reason emerges now.

As previously stated, Benasayag noted that there is now a sort of hybridization, interpenetration, and overall unity between the concepts of functioning and existing (p. 19). Such intersections entail the metaphorical decline of human existence, often reduced to predictive models, algorithms, calculations, and computerization.[13] In the words of Benasayag (2019, p. 10):

> The dimensions and processes of existence are exactly those of the living, of culture, those for which the questions of meaning, negativity and non-knowing remain central: experience is not reducible to the collection of information; the exploration of possibilities by the living is something quite different from the search for performance, the path of a life has nothing to do with a career plan.

The complexity of human beings (partially mysterious and unpredictable), their irreducibility to calculated programming,[14] and their simultaneous immersion in the digital world has yielded a split between the need for absolute efficiency (typical of the machine perspective) and the unavoidable limits of the biographical aspects of life (typical of existential logic).

Productivity and efficiency are fundamental aspects of our age that cause violent and continuous existential stress. Further, relationships are fragile in this panorama, and this phenomenon increasingly characterizes our being in the world. Finally, we can state that the contemporary dogma of the need for absolute measurement and control (typical of functioning logic) constitutes a particularly fertile ground for the development of anxiety and mood disorders (contrary to the logic of existence).

---

[13] "Today we could speak of 'modular man': an individual from whom useless modules are eliminated to replace them with useful modules" (Benasayag, 2019, p. 56).

[14] "What kind of society is it that no longer attributes any value to the sculpture of life, which is sculpture of bodies, of the memory of bodies, of experience, of wounds, of powers?" (Benasayag, 2019, p. 19). The human being is, therefore, a field of possibilities that cannot be reduced to pure functioning but constantly refers to the unrepeatable situations in which he or she takes root, in which each of us, with continuous modifications and adjustments, carves our own life (which is made of dynamic singularities set in concrete situations). Here a suggestive reference emerges, in the form of biographical-existential sculpture, to the powerful metaphor of the Plotinian statue: "act as does the creator of a statue that is to be made beautiful: he cuts away here, he smoothes there, he makes this line lighter, this other purer, until a lovely face has grown upon his work. So do you also: cut away all that is excessive, straighten all that is crooked, bring light to all that is overcast, labour to make all one glow of beauty and never cease chiselling your statue, until there shall shine out on you from it the godlike splendour of virtue" (see Plotinus, *Enneads*, I, 6,9,7).

I.3   THE EXISTENTIAL VIEWS OF CONTEMPORARY HUMANITY

Considering previous theories, we can identify three existential per-spectives that symbolize the dynamics of anxious and depressed hypermodern human beings:

- *At urbulent and confusing conception of time.* According to Merlini, many people live within a time dimension that is "atomized" or void of duration: thus, everything in our life appears transitory, ephemeral, and momentary. This shift to a perception of time wherein rhythm and order are lacking can cause people to feel as though their power to act and their potential for action are diminished.[15] Such a depressing worldview can force the human ego to become self-referential and make the body the ultimate meaning of all existence (see Gabrielli and Garlaschelli, 2016). The obsession with a healthy, efficient, and productive body renders the idea of death increasingly difficult to accept,[16] including the many metaphorical deaths (our failures)[17] that pervade our existence (from affective sorrows to missed job targets). Consequently, this dynamic also often makes it difficult for people to accept their senility, instilling the feeling that they never really become old (see Han, 2017a). According to Gabrielli, a type of "militarization of the body" now dominates because of the obsession with the aesthetic dimension to gain maximum social visibility. There exist two extremes: people who are severely self-disciplined and those who abuse compulsive pleasures and addictions (see Gabrielli, Garlaschelli, and Guarracino, 2017). Finally, we can assert that the anthropological panorama is now often inhabited by numerous narcissistic dynamics related to short-term relationships and fragile emotional ties. In such narcissistic relationships, pathos and intensity are deemed more important than the duration of the relationship itself. All these processes correlate with anti-community forms of tribal entrenchment (for instance, food tribes, as we

---

[15]   In the everyday frenzy there is the ideal profile of efficiency, which translates into the uncontrolled increase of the imbalance between available time resources and tasks to be fulfilled (see Merlini, 2019).

[16]   As Han (2017a) maintains, the right time or the right moment emerges only within a relationship of temporal tension: in atomized time, instead, the moments are equal to each other and nothing distinguishes them from each other.

[17]   Today, death is seen almost as an unnatural event, constituting instead a rewarding mystery to be always considered (see Minkowski, 2004).

will see) (see Aceranti, Gabrielli, and Cocchi, 2013; Gabrielli, Carta, and De Filippo, 2016).

- *The self-centered individual* (see Han, 2015b; Ehrenberg, 1999; Gabrielli, 2012, 2014). We transitioned from a disciplinary society expressive of obligations and prohibitions to a society wherein successful performance is imperative in all facets of life (see Ehrenberg, 1999). The individual is only apparently free (because of the belief of mastery over personal initiatives); in reality, societies often push individuals to their highest performance levels until they burn out. A brutal process is apparent in all such processes: human beings are seen as successful only when they are productive; their value decreases when they are no longer productive. In such scenarios, therefore, human beings are obsessed with productivity, and when they are exhausted and no longer efficient, they feel invisible, cut off from the social context, and ashamed of their inadequacy. Shame is now the desecration of one's self-esteem, and it is the ideal background for the proliferation of depression; this tendency is coherent with contemporary narcissistic culture (see Han, 2017b and Petrosino, 2015).
- *Confusion between fundamental human needs and desires.* Confusion and difficulties now arise in the distinctions between anxieties engendered by basic human needs and desires. Lacan distinguished the concepts of desire and need and said that desire reveals our shortcomings. Desire indicates human limits, while need pushes human beings to find optimal fulfilling strategies (for example, to find the tools to satisfy a need and calm anxiety). Lacan configured desire as a more mysterious concept because of which human beings are never completely satisfied. It is perpetually elusive, ungovernable, obscure, and inevitable (see Han, 2017b).

Finally, we can note that desire appears to human beings as the sensation of knowing they are missing something but are unaware of what precisely is lacking in their lives. Instead, we are aware of what we want when we fulfill a need: for example, we need to eat, so we want food when we feel hungry; if we cannot eat for an extended period of time, we become anxious. Both need and desire are essential. However, according to Lacan, desire is very significant because it is the basis of creative logic. We can satisfy a need (for example, by eating); however, we cannot satisfy desire. Therefore, we sublimate desire through the creative arts: desire is the source of creativity. With regard to this, Lacan (2006) writes that when we talk of desire, we indicate an existential "lack of being": Desire, a function central to all human experience, is the desire for nothing nameable. And at the same time this desire lies at the origin of every variety of animation. If being were only what it is, there wouldn't even be room to talk about it. Being comes into existence as an exact function of this lack. According to Lacan, an unbridgeable emptiness infuses our existence and stimulates our creativity (through our attempts to fill the emptiness). This process of research, animated by desire, is never fully sated precisely because it is not the dynamic of a need (which can be fulfilled, as is the case with hunger).

Within desire exists restlessness and a sort of tension to transcend the egocentrism of one's needs. In desire, we can find the impulse to abandon the self-referential narcissistic logic (which sees other human beings as objects to satisfy one's own needs). Desire elicits excitement about life; this drive of desire makes it possible to live in real relationships with other people without using them.[18]

Even when human beings realize the maximum potential of the satisfaction of their needs, they feel the presence of something different: the desire that can never be satisfied and that always remains within them. According to Lacan, being aware of the constant and unappeasable presence of desire allows us to discover ourselves as limited beings and to recognize our finiteness (and the finiteness of all other human beings). This process permits the recognition of a common human aspect and enables people to care about and respect the individuality of others, an inexhaustible ethical task. Respecting other human beings and not using people as tools for the satisfaction of one's needs means surmounting the contemporary narcissistic logic. This rationale views people as objects to be used for one's own purposes and needs, whereas it is important to go beyond the perverse and anxious dynamics of the continual satisfaction of one's needs. Therefore, it is necessary to discover a stable point in our epoch,

[18] Lacan (2006). On this issue, see the incisive study by Petrosino (2019).

defined as "liquid" (and which can even be described as an era without character).[19]

1.4   AN ERA METAPHORICALLY "CROSSED BY WATER"

Scholars ranging from Luigi Pirandello to Zygmunt Bauman have described the twentieth century as a time metaphorically "crossed by water." The century was representative of fluidity in terms of projects, world visions, and bonds; during this time, human civilizations could no longer exemplify a solid and reassuring image of the earth (Pirandello, 1960).

Pirandello articulated a prophetic intuition about this liquid social dynamic:

> In certain moments of turmoil, all these fictitious forms are hit by the flux and collapse miserably under its thrust; and even that which does not flow under the barrier and beyond the limits, that which is distinctly clear to us and which we have carefully channeled into our feelings, into the duties we have imposed upon ourselves, into the habit we have marked out or ourselves, in certain moments of floodtide, overflows and upsets everything.
>
> *(1960, pp. 151–152)*

Certainly, some dissipation and disintegration dynamics can now be observed; we can also observe liquescence and instability within work environments, communities, and social relationships. Therefore, we can note the end of certain social systems along with their traditional well-correlated and defined roles. Currently, relationships are fragile; Luhmann (1979) observed that the old symbolism of people as travelers or pilgrims is disappearing, and a new metaphor of the vagabond or the tourist is now being established. According to Natoli (2010), a person is, at the same time, everywhere and nowhere. This shift is typified by "atomized time" that displays an eternal present.

---

[19]   Petrosino (2019); see also Lévinas (1990). For a historical–theoretical framework of the phenomenological–hermeneutical approach, see Gabrielli and Garlaschelli (2017, 2018) and Schmitt (1999).

Zygmunt Bauman[20] highlighted the failure of the Freudian *Sicherheit* (security, certainty, and safety) because the following features are now evident:

– the loss of existential security
– the loss of certainty
– the loss of personal safety

This condition of insecurity and widespread precariousness can frequently cause the emergence of other aspects: a sort of victimhood, emotional indifference, psychological amplification of the narcissistic ego, fragile relationships, and fascination with extreme situations (see Bauman, 2000 and Glaeßner, 2002).

Sennett (1999) believed that the frenetic and changeable hypermodern capitalism could cause a collapse of human identity; thus, an individual devoid of character and personality often materializes, incapable of healthy relationships (as suggested by the etymological and semantic outline of the term "character").[21]

Present-day individuals are often overwhelmed by brief excitement, consumerism, and emotional indifference (see Sennett, 1999). Such people are incapable of conducting a life that is based on the virtues of firmness and constancy, which are expressions of character (Han, 2019, p. 62)

Frequently, in a world without character, there is no space for beauty, responsibility, or forms of seduction capable of promoting

---

[20]   The "pointillist time," proper to the technological society, is inhabited by incoherence; devoid of cohesion; divided into eternal moments disconnected from each other; and bound to the ideology of the present, immediate use, pleasure, excess, and unabated performance (Bauman, 2010). See also Maffesoli (2003) and Aubert (2003).

[21]   The term "character" derives from the Greek *charassein*, meaning digging, engraving, impressing, and then establishing something firm, a limit, in our case, the stable, lasting sign, capable of engraving our capabilities and our projects (see Lasch, 1985). Schmitt (1999, p. 20) praises "character" in this sense: the stability of the earth in comparison to the lack of delimitation and measure, the absence of stability and character of the sea. D. Hume (1971, vol. I) spoke of pride, which is not arrogance or presumption but awareness of one's qualities and limits, not only recognition of one's irreplaceable uniqueness and of how people realize themselves but also possession of an extreme sense of proportion, that of the right measure. See also Natoli (1997).

passion, reliable ideas, durability, and loyalty to projects. What do we mean by "beauty"?

> In order to change the paradigm of the human body image ... the proposed shift should be from a hedonistic male functionalism and the commercialized ... to the aesthetics and beauty.
>
> Beauty implies more than physicality. It refers to the representation of meaning and the body as the evidence of grace and humane nobility. The proportions of the body and the harmony of body wholeness project beauty.
>
> *(Louw, 2017, p. 47)*

In our hypermodern context, there are often no human bonds rooted in stability, and there is no attention devoted to the profound contemplation of beauty because perpetual excitement is commonly observed as occurring along with the associated compulsive consumerism: all is exchangeable and precarious while correlated to a stubborn tyranny of the present.[22]

Hartmut Rosa posited that the current human perception of time acceleration is attributable only to the extreme speed of life in the present and its productive processes. The fear of not fully consuming all the possibilities of life and the fear of not living "the beauty of life" emerge from these dynamics. Synthetically, we can affirm that one now has to act fast to enjoy every option that life has to offer:

> The fear of missing out on things, options, and consequently the desire to intensify the pace of life are the result of a cultural project developed in modern times, which consists in making one's life

---

[22] For an overview, see Zamperini (2007), Pulcini (2001), and Han (2017c). According to Lipovetsky (2019), even if the society of seduction, as it works these days, does not provide us with the means to satisfactorily deal with the challenges of the future and requires in this respect different counterweights, we must not demonize this kingdom. It is the new society of seduction that frees us from the hegemony of materialistic and presentist values. It is compatible with commitment and work, self-surpassing, creation, and reflection. Our responsibility is to promote increased seduction, that is, seduction capable of giving impetus to rich and good passions, and which allows the development of oneself and the enrichment of human experiences and faculties.

fuller and fuller through accelerations, by multiplying one's lived experiences, to achieve a supposed "good life."

(Rosa, 2005, p. 218)

In reality, the perpetual acceleration and speed of life are not the problem; often the present-day relationship with time is concerning as it is frequently characterized by a disorienting anxiety, an incapacity to serenely live time and govern it; thus, one can observe the inability to recognize beauty intensively, as the true perception of beauty requires calm and serene contemplation

Human beings manifest an inability to linger and experience duration:

When we are constantly asked to renew ourselves, to choose a new option or version of a product, we may get the impression that life is accelerating. In reality, what we face is an absence of any experience of duration ... The impression that time moves considerably faster than in the past originates from the fact that today we are unable to linger, and that the experience of duration has become rare.

It is mistakenly assumed that the feeling of being rushed is the result of a "fear of missing out." The fear of not being able to enjoy valuable things, and therefore the desire to heighten the pace of life, are the result of a cultural program that began developing in early modernity.

This cultural project consists in making one's own life fulfilled and richer in experiences ... i.e. by escalating the number of experiences and thereby realizing a "good life." The cultural promise of acceleration is rooted in this idea; as a result individuals want to live faster.

(Han, 2017a, pp. 43–44)

No stillness is commonly perceived in the present, only oppressive and pressing time dimensions. We now meet the timeless individual for whom everything is calculation and breathlessness. This kind of person considers everything without a narrative continuity, without history, without memory. In this accelerated time dimension, there seems to be no space for things that are complex, mysterious, indefinite, and innumerable.[23] Thus, there is no possibility of comprehending the innumerable shades of human life in its existence and its shadows. Frequently, there is no space for tenderness, affection, and feelings (Han, 2017a). In this hypermodern process, there is often no quiet time, no wonder, and no occasion to be surprised. We are often unable to sense astonishment because this feeling cannot exist in the "atomized time dimension," a sort of breathless time that is devoid of tension and dialectics. According to Petrosino, the immediate present trait that it is crucial to examine is that of surprise because its manifestation requires time to wonder, linger, and live fully and mindfully (see Petrosino, 2012 and Cocchi et al., 2016). Nowadays, this ability is rare.

This is a time for the most part that is incapable of delays; a hypervigilant era resistant to surprise. Often, people live with a subtle and invasive malaise and display an ambiguous (if not pathological) relationship with their bodies and with food (see Gabrielli et al., 2015). According to de Sutter (2018), forms of induced excitement and sedation are commonly used and aimed at downsizing different types of anxiety that are increasing and widespread.

In this present efficiency-obsessed society, all is focused on high performance; the human ego has replaced the past importance of duty with the contemporary significance of power (see Han, 2015b). This transferal occurs not because the human being is free (i.e., has the power to be free) but because freedom is only apparent. Han (2015b)

---

[23] For an overview, see Han (2017a). Presentism generates an empty form, a *blank duration*. Th. W. Adorno (1974, p. 165) writes with suggestive gait: "Sleepless night: so there is a formula for those tormented hours, drawn out without prospect of end or dawn, in the vain effort to forget time's empty passing. But truly terrifying are the sleepless nights when time seems to contract and run fruitlessly through our hands ... But what is revealed in such contraction of the hours is the reverse of time fulfilled. If in the latter the power of experience breaks the spell of duration and gathers past and future into the present, in the hasteful sleepless night duration causes unendurable dread."

(commenting on Foucault) maintains that human beings are paradox-ically (and falsely) free in the current circumstances: individuals have become obedient to the diktat "be free; you can," by means of which technological society imposes productivity to the point of burnout (i.e., you can produce nonstop, until you reach a state of physical or emotional exhaustion). In this situation, the hyper-powered narcissis-tic dynamic emerges and frequently leads human beings to depression. Every biographical project becomes a sort of interrupted narration in this process – timeless and without history.

Therefore, the sovereign ego, violently free, is the architect of not only its self-affirmation but also its defeat and is unable to forgive or be grateful. This ego becomes filled with shame when it does not receive approval from an external source, or worse, it disdains what it cannot actualize (not being able to realize something generates guilt) (see Han, 2018). There is an overflow of shame into depression in this dynamic.[24] In this regard, Alain Ehrneberg stated in a well-known book, *La Fatigue d'être soi* [Tired of being oneself] (1999), that in the age of technology, the individual is at risk of falling into depression because of constant exposure to obsessive demands for efficiency and adequacy (by many existential and professional situations). Depression has attained new forms in the era of technology.[25] It is no longer characterized by the ancient classical neurotic conflict between norm and transgression; it is now typified by a vigorous

---

[24] Shame has changed its face in our age, to the extent that it has become unselfish toward itself: in a society centered entirely on the performance of the narcissistic subject, every failure can only be ascribed to oneself, hence the shame of not having been up to the task. See Turnaturi (2012).

[25] The current technological times celebrate the imperative to consume everything at once, because the opportunities that present themselves today will never present themselves to you again. They emphasize a hyper-strengthened voluntarism and an exasperated activism because in a world perceived as imponderable, precarious, and inhospitable, it is considered necessary to control uncertainty obsessively in order to survive and at the same time to frantically devour every fragment of existence. In summary, we live in the so-called contingency age: The era of globalization is also a time of contingency. The two phenomena are connected to one another and mark a profound transformation in the horizons of life and in the crucial elements of modernity. For an overview, see also Mongardini (2009) and Gabrielli (2012).

feeling of inadequacy, implying our passage from a society of guilt (according to Ehrenberg, 2019[26]) to one of responsibility and initiative.

When initiative becomes a fundamental ideal within a society, and contemporary reality is lived only through a sense of distressing precariousness and a longing for the satisfaction of desire, that society is not considered adequate for the achievement of the aforementioned standards, and individuals lose their importance as a human being (see Han, 2018). This principle correlates with the fatigue of living, the anguish of always being inadequate, and the consequent sense of potential latent existential failure.

Depression has become a typical pathology of our times; it is the disease of personal motivation, a state without projects, and a condition filled with inhibition. Anguish has now changed its blueprint:

> Many people today are affected by widespread anxieties: anguish about not succeeding, about failure, about becoming dependent, anguish about making mistakes or of making a wrong decision, anguish about not being able to meet one's needs. Such anxieties are made ever greater by constantly comparing oneself to others.
>
> *(Han, 2019, p. 46)*

We have now become our own managers, self-employed and mere subjects of performance, following the extreme efficiency principle of endless calculation. Frequently, we are isolated in an atomized time (time without duration) where we need to affirm ourselves at an obsessive speed.[27] People often follow a standardized scheme and

---

26   Ehrenberg (2019) actually sees a certain complementarity between depression and dependence: Depression is the degeneration of an individual who is only himself and, consequently, never himself, as if he is perpetually running after his own shadow. If depression is the pathology of a consciousness that is only itself, dependence is the pathology of a consciousness that is never sufficiently itself, never sufficiently full of identity, never sufficiently active, because it is too indecisive, too explosive. Depression and addiction are like the obverse and the reverse of the same failure condition.

27   For a view of how the cult of celebrity and the accumulation of fame also depend on speed, see Hillman (2001).

consumerist behavior. This dynamic brings tormented distress caused by fear of failure within an eternal, inescapable present. The consequent feeling is of inadequacy in the face of the infinite tasks that must be accomplished every day. This sense of insufficiency can trigger social anxiety (see Bude, 2014).

1.5   THE BODY WITHOUT DECENCY: A CONTEMPORARY PHENOMENA

It can finally be asserted that in the current scenario, the following holds true: "In the social media, film, many magazines and public advertisements, the naked human body is often projected as a commodity and portrayed as object for lust and sexual gratification" (Louw, 2017, p. 41). Naked, perfect, seductive, and smooth bodies are used today to advertise everything, and this is not a coincidence. We live in an era of extreme metaphorical transparency where everything is smooth, flat, linear, flexible, adaptable, and devoid of obstacles or resistance (like Jeff Koons' sculptures and certain smartphones) (see Han, 2017c).

> This shift towards a more aesthetic approach to human life is even detectable in processes of high-tech digitalisation and information technology with its emphasis on "big data." Man is also the creator of beauty: man as *homo aestheticus*. For example, Steve Jobs, the digital entrepreneur of Apple, introduced aesthetics to the computer business. He combined his slogan "Let's make a dent in the universe" with the aesthetics and art of design. While his youth companion Steve Wozniak could see "a sonnet in a circuit," Jobs, by contrast, could look at a beige box and see beauty. "He imagined a computer that was graceful and elegant as it was useful, an intersection of technology and art that resulted in something truly special."
>
> Steve Jobs changed a possible bankrupt company, Apple, into a financial miracle. The secret? He stayed true to his original vision for Apple: He believed there was room for beauty and art amid technology and commerce.

(Louw, 2017, p. 41)

This conception is typical of the current era. According to Gadamer, it must also meet both the positive and the negative aspects of life. This was particularly true of the past when art promoted beauty and celebrated otherness, which was never fully controllable. All that is obscure and raw must be represented by art to illustrate the "aesthetic of the wound."[28]

> All is now changed; art frequently reproduces our bodies with an emphasis on smoothness, transparency, and perfection (see Han, 2015c). From this perspective, bodies are made public; they are made naked, bereft of veils and secrets, standardized, and sculpted with uniforming techniques (plastic surgery and Photoshop). Human bodies are frequently shown in their extreme nakedness, without character, and without signs of aging. They are represented by anonymous images without shame.[29] Conversely, modesty and decency are opposed to transparency and vulgarity but are matched with reservation (see Han, 2015a), delicacy, uniqueness, and dignity. These features recall the body as a mystery in order to safeguard its singularity. Modesty promotes the erotic component of the body, not its pornography: the myth of Eros inhabits the hiding place, the crypt, the enigma; on the contrary pornography loves the spotlight, in which everything is smooth, flat, shiny, nothing is hidden or mysterious.

Louw describes, how through the impact of the media, the human body has been instrumentalized and commodified.

> nudity becomes commercialized: gratuitous nudity. Nudity has become naturalized to such an extent that advertisements of

---

[28] Gadamer (1988, p. 37) states, in this context, that art invites us to change our lives: "You must change your life. It is a shock, being shaken at the roots, which takes place precisely through the particularity in which every artistic experience presents itself."

[29] On modesty as a fruitful space of freedom against today's dictatorship of transparency, of the extreme smoothness of experiences and actions, see Selz (2005). See also Scheler (1979) on feelings of modesty as "a turning back to the self."

half-transparent underwear revealing the genitals have become normal; they have become cultural products.

(Louw, 2017, p. 53)

While eroticism seeks respect for mystery and secrets, conversely, pornography claims homogeneity and the spotlight: "Nothing is more homogeneous than a pornographic photograph ... Just like a window display illuminating a single jewel. Pornographic photographs are entirely concerned with the exposition of one thing only – sex" (Barthes, 1980, p. 42). The pornography of bodies, their marked visibility and extreme exposure, their confinement to a sole purpose of enjoyment and pleasure,[30] their amplification of sensationalism, and their undue metaphoric equation of nudity[31] have probably and partially contributed to the contemporary difficulties in the relationship with the body. They are thus correlated with some pathologies as we will see in subsequent sections.

In social media, there is the real danger that the naked human body is exploited for commercial gain. Advertisements often leave the impression that the body, very specifically the genitals, is designed merely for physical desire and corporeal chemistry. They become easily objects for lust, excluded from the beauty of graceful existence and noble courage. It is argued that the naked human body is not designed for pornographic exploitation and promiscuous sensuality but for compassionate intimacy and nurturing care in order to instill a humane dimension in human and sexual encounters. In this regard, antiquity and the Michelangelesque perspective can contribute to a paradigm shift from abusive exploitation to the beauty of vulnerable sensitivity (Louw, 2017, p. 41).

---

[30]   On the concept of pleasure, see Žižek (2009) and Petrosino (2013).

[31]   Perhaps nobody more than J.-L. Nancy knew how to grasp the highest human figure in the nudity of the skin, in its resistance to every form of truthful disclosure, in its exposure, and in contact as a place of the relationship. For an overview, see Nancy (2008).

PART II Brain without Body, Body without Brain, and Contemporary Body Image Disorders

2   Body Schema, Body Image, and Hypermodern Alterations

2.1   BRAIN WITHOUT BODY: ABSTRACTIZATION

The ego is first and foremost a body-ego.

(Freud, 1923, p. 27)

The epistemological debate about the relationship between mind and body is ancient. Nevertheless, the present focus on the body is new and highly topical precisely because of the importance accorded by contemporary cultures to the corporeal dimension, particularly to body image. In fact, the systematic study of the body as representation was initiated only at the beginning of this century (see Molinari and Castelnuovo, 2012).

For a long time, multidisciplinary research exerted very little influence on the development of theories; it is only in the past few years that factors closely related to bodily experiences, such as the spread of eating disorders,[1] have prompted researchers to a greater conceptual systematization. In sum, the scientific process caused the inclusion of the perceptual, affective, and cognitive representations of the human body to be divided into two fundamental and intertwined concepts: body schema and body image (Molinari and Castelnuovo, 2012).

---

[1] Dissatisfaction and discomfort with respect to one's body are key symptoms of eating disorders and are found in other psychiatric syndromes as well. For example, obesity-related studies on body image disorders and their relationships with dietary styles are increasing. For an overview, see Molinari and Castelnuovo (2012).

What do we mean by these terms?

- Body schema comprises the representation of the neurological and perceptual patterns of the body.[2]
- Body image, on the other hand, refers to emotional and cognitive representations.[3] It is closely linked to emotional reality, relationships with significant relational human figures, and personal history. Body image is also a reality that changes over time; further, it is generated and reorganized because of external stimuli. This process occurs at varying levels: emotional, imaginary, sensory, and creative.[4] The analysis of body image is therefore not a neurological[5] but primarily a psychological issue because it involves emotional and existential situations, past memories, and personal motivations. Body image can be influenced by the experiences of life both in the most intimate interpersonal relationships and in the broader social and cultural context. It can be noted that the following holds true:

> Body image is a multidimensional construct that refers to one's perception of and attitudes about the size and shape of one's body. It has both a perceptual component that refers to how we see our body size, shape, weight, physical characteristics, performance, and movement, and an evaluative component, which refers to how we

[2]   The concept of a body schema includes very different processes and experiences. Although no pathology can destroy the body schema, more pathologies are capable of altering some features of this scheme. Some areas of the brain functionally linked to the body schema have been identified in recent years. A process of spatial localization performed by the nervous system occurs, and sensory inputs are processed several times in different brain areas. In this regard, Schilder (1973) states that we receive sensations, see part of the surface of our body, have tactile and thermal impressions, but beyond these processes is the immediate experience of the existence of bodily unity that is more than a single perception. For further information, see Molinari and Castelnuovo (2012).

[3]   Some authors have criticized the use of such broad concepts because they include very different experiences; however, scientists often recognize the need to use conventionally common references to allow exchange between different disciplines to occur. See Molinari and Castelnuovo (2012).

[4]   To be precise, Schilder (1973) defines the body image as how our body appears to us. This perception includes the personal experience of our body. For an overview, see Molinari and Castelnuovo (2012).

[5]   Gallagher (2005) states that it is important to make a distinction because the terms "body image" and "body schema," which are often confused, creating a methodological and conceptual uncertainty. We need to keep this distinction between the two constructs in mind.

feel about these attributes and how those feelings influence our behaviors.

(Mills, Shannon, and Hogue, 2017, p. 146)

It makes sense at this point to note that the most intimate relationships, along with the social and cultural context, can significantly affect these subjective representations.[6] In fact, it is known that the human mind is created and takes shape owing to interactions between mental processes related to inner reality (neurophysiological processes) and experiences related to external reality (i.e., those experienced in interpersonal interactions,[7] social situations, and contact with the surrounding habitat). These reciprocal influences between external dimensions and inner realities contribute to the shaping of the common development of nerve connections, which engenders the mind. The mind is a stream of information that "creates representations"[8] such as the body schema and the body image.

In recent decades, scientific research has accorded increasing importance to the interactive and relational components of the subject's psychological experience (see Acquati and Saita, 2017; Durbano, 2018). It is necessary for this context to emphasize that both intimate relationships and the wider social environment, which mass media can aptly represent, affect human perceptions:

> It could be that the mass media affect their audience not only by reinforcing beauty ideals ("thin is beautiful") or by eliciting immediate changes in terms of how people perceive and evaluate their own appearance but also by influencing perceived norms.

---

[6]   This concept is, in turn, intertwined with the concept of body schema.

[7]   The development of brain structures and functions depends on how experiences, in particular, those related to interpersonal relationships, influence and shape the genetically determined maturation programs of the nervous system. For further details, see Siegel (2013).

[8]   In the form of neuronal excitation patterns. For an overview, see footnote 7. See also Cavalli (2017).

Experimental findings demonstrate that perceptions of what is considered to be "average" influence how individuals feel about their own bodies.

In other words, one of the reasons that media-portrayed thin ideal images can be harmful is because they skew what people think of as being "normal" or typical in a given population.

(Mills et al., 2017, p. 149)

This scenario is very complex because we know that if the external habitat affects the individual, the subject also influences the surrounding environment in turn; therefore, very intricate circles of mutual influence are created. Sander (2007) and before him Janet (1929) speak in this regard of a sort of integrative function that, in the flow of our involvement with the environment, provides human beings with the fundamental motivation to "put everything together." People can thus create coherence and face this complexity (i.e., integrate many different and interacting messages that emanate from their inner and outer realities).

According to Janet (1929, p. 16), this function of synthesis seems to discharge a "unifying role" for the subject: "The personality is presented to us as an internal work, and not just as an external work ... a process to unify and to distinguish oneself" (see also Silvestri, 2015). Therefore, in Sander's (2007) words, we can see ordering thrusts that allow "the organization of an almost infinite complexity in a single coherent unit" (p. 216). Fortunately, the potential to manage complexity and find unity and coherence is implicitly a human characteristic, but some specific questions now arise on the matter of how far this human potential to manage the constant hypermodern complexity can be pushed and how an individual is presently solicited in the construction of self-representation, particularly bodily.

So much of external reality (both in terms of relationships and, more generally, in terms of habitat) has now changed, thanks to the many inventions that have radically revolutionized human life throughout history. To exemplify, humans learned how to change the cycle of nature with the discovery of plows and no longer needed to wander in search of new resources. The breeding and domestication of animals accompanied this sedentarization process, and at around the same time, human beings tamed fire. Then, they no longer had to wait for lightning to burn a tree to heat themselves. These changes offered humanity new agencies. These revolutions enhanced the human ability to manage reality; thus, reality seemed to simplify. Everything appeared more comfortable and orderly in the life of the sedentary human; people bred and cultivated, heated food with fire, and protected themselves more readily against cold winters.

Humanity has aspired for millennia, therefore, to liberate itself from nature's constraints, using ever more sophisticated technologies and artifacts, to which more and more tasks have been delegated. Initially, the creation of artifact tools was aimed at a single concrete purpose: simplifying life. The plow was created, designed, and used for a single purpose that was clear, specific, simple, unique, and defined: plowing. The resulting crops then simplified everyday life. An artifact made sense as long as it served its single purpose. The tool was useful, it had value, and its value was equal to its usage for its purpose. The plow was not abstracted (see Irtelli, 2019).

What do we mean by this term? Today, products are often abstracted because of discrete marketing operations. They are increasingly widespread, and their presence is decreasingly linked to their actual use. Nowadays, artifact tools are designed to represent expressions of social or individual identity (see Blythe and Cedrola, 2013). No longer is a simple object sold. What is increasingly offered for sale is a personality or an attractive lifestyle.

Our hypermodern culture is indeed characterized by fast production and consumption. It is focused on market needs and industrial production rather than the actual requirements of a real person. This trend models the industrial production of market needs and does not foreground the human dimension. It is an expression of the mechanism of abstractization, which permeates market logic, such that both the inner and the outer perceptions become abstract. Similarly, the goods sold on the market have become increasingly abstract. The contact with real experiences and the things we buy has been lost in a sense. The relationships of people with their five senses, and more generally, their associations with their bodies, have also congruently transformed, perhaps along with the representations people develop for themselves.

We cite a few examples to better elucidate this concept. Perfume advertisements denote clear examples of abstractization. Almost no mention is made of the product's olfactory notes, how it is conceived, its manufacturing process, or the specific fragrance offered for sale. Conversely, commercials tend to present a fantastical and unreal story to promote its use and elicit the need to possess it. They reference a kind of abstract icon or a lifestyle that is completely unrelated to the fragrance and how it smells. The perfume's characteristics remain largely unknown (see Irtelli, 2019).

Therefore, an unreal concept almost totally separated from the product offered for purchase is communicated. An experience that has little connection with what has been offered (i.e., the perfumed liquid within the bottle) is promised. Ultimately, an abstract idea that actually has little or nothing to do with the product is provided.

This fact does not apply just to perfumes: numerous products are now sold through the representation of unreal experiences. Fantastic narratives are transmitted as phenomena connected to the product while not actually associated with the product's features.

To clarify this point, the purchase of something, therefore, occurs on the basis of feelings that are unrelated to the actual experience of that something or with its usefulness (see Blythe and Cedrola, 2013). An object's practical function (watch, mobile phone, perfume, T-shirt, etc.) and the bodily experience linked to its utility often become secondary. However, the abstract message thought to be communicated by means of possessing that particular thing is increasingly highlighted.

The second example relates to sweatshirts, now designed and sold mainly for their use in dressing up and protecting the body, with the process of making and designing them becoming progressively less creative. More frequently, the product reveals the social status, life-style, and sometimes even the ideologies of the wearer. The artifact becomes an expression of something else, and the choice of a product is commonly linked to meanings, ideals, and symbols, leading to the process of abstractization (Blythe and Cedrola, 2013).

The five senses are, therefore, often subverted by marketing logic, creating artificial connections. A sophisticated multisensory involvement of the individual is sought to attract people to purchase a product. People are allured by products through diverse stratagems to push the act of purchase. Such sensory engagements to induce people to buy an item on offer could include music (even when the product does not emit sound), fragrances (although they are unrelated to the use of the relevant artifact), color (even if it is marginal in the use of the artifact, for example, in phones), and symbols of various kinds. To summarize, a sort of manipulation now transpires, leading to the loss of contact with the real experience of that "something" for which it occurs.

Third, we allude to a big store offering expensive items of cloth-ing. The music is very loud (as in a discotheque) in this store; the salespeople usually dance in the dim lights; it is difficult to adequately view the textile of the clothes that one will buy. However, numerous people are engaged in the creation of an exciting atmosphere, and a strong, sophisticated perfume is diffused on purpose to devise a mix of sensations that stimulate the purchase of a product scarcely visible in the dim lighting. Nevertheless, many people like this store, particularly because it is full of idealized significations that incite people to think as people do when they are overwhelmed by euphoria (see Irtelli, 2019).

Some sensory, cognitive, and individual emotional responses are activated in this process of abstractization and are combined in an attempt to penetrate the human mind in order to develop lasting results through certain manipulated mental representations. Behavioral economics studies view human beings as a set of brain behaviors and functions to be conditioned, penetrated, and shaped, often wresting them away from the true perception of phenomena as they exist in reality.

2.2 MECHANIZATION

> You can read on Wikipedia about the well-known Eugene Goostman who, in June 2012, ranked first in Milton Keynes, taking part in the largest event ever organized for conducting a Turing test. He talks about his life, and he claims, to anyone who asks him, to be a thirteen-year-old Ukrainian living in Odessa, with a gynecologist father, a homemaker mother, and a guinea pig. Eugene chats.
>
> Veselov stated that Eugene Goostman, who is only thirteen, was devised precisely for the purpose of acquiring "a credible personality"; according to Veselov at the age of thirteen, after all, one is "neither too old to know everything, nor too young to not know anything." His young age also entails minor grammatical errors in his answers, and this is completely understandable.
>
> In 2014, his capability to dialogue was improved, and in the future, the logic with which his conversations are conducted will also be improved.
>
> Eugene does not sleep and has not eaten since forever.
>
> In the experiments, Eugene even persuades about a third of the judges to believe him to be a human.
>
> Eugene has no organs, no soul, but travels on the internet.
>
> Eugene is a chatterbox.[9]

> (Irtelli, 2019, pp. 21–22)

Presently, the trend of mechanization accompanies the aforementioned phenomenon of abstractization. In this context, Miguel Benasayag (2015) reckons that a sort of hybridization is now occurring between man and machine. The creation of a mix between man and

---

[9]   On June 7, 2014, the sixtieth anniversary of Turing's death, 33 percent of the judges of the Turing test believed that Goostman was a human. Event organizer Kevin Warwick recalls that Turing had predicted that by the year 2000, computers would be able to convince 30 percent of tested humans after five minutes of conversation. Critics discussed the validity and relevance of the passing of the Turing test by Goostman, particularly in relation to the media bomb launched by the event organizer, Kevin Warwick. For further details, see Irtelli (2019).

machine that goes beyond the already existent enhancement is well underway. Benasayag postulates a transformation effected via an arti-fact–organism hybridization. In essence, mechanization is viewed as the manufacture of a combination of the human brain and an artifact.[10]

To exemplify this phenomenon, several neurophysiological researchers have realized that the brain modifies its architecture when a familiar video game is played: the prefrontal zones thicken. Players were delighted when this news was announced, but the second part of this information was missing: studies on the development of intelligence showed that these areas shrink in size in the development of intelligence and that the opposite is not the case (see Benasayag, 2015).

Many types of human–machine hybridizations are presented through the simple delegation of cognitive functions to technology. Such combinations relate to the formation of actual circuits and neurophysiological loops that result in a mix without the need to implant an artifact into the human body, contrary to sci-fi representations.

We can cite another peculiar example apropos mechanization, a phenomenon that is presently becoming widespread: smartphone applications aiming to support individuals in moments of psychic pain (one such application actually includes a word representing psy-chic suffering in its name: Woe).[11] A yellow robot appears in one application and exclaims, "Hi!" It holds a folder in his hands, and during the so-called conversations, it projects short videos dressed in a doctor-like white coat, stating that it will help the user via Cognitive Behavioral Therapy, which is scientifically proven to work. The robot suggests to the human subject during the chat to directly enter responses to its statements. It is not even necessary for people to

---

[10]   Anatomical modification of the phenotype of the brain. For more details, see Benasayag (2018).

[11]   The name (Woe) is not a randomly selected term because it means moral pain; it is not, in fact, pain as in physical discomfort.

cognize their answers because the robot thinks of the possible replies in lieu of human users, who are thus relieved of the responsibility for reasoning. Prepackaged potential responses appear on-screen and can be clicked on without any effort: users need not think about their views; they must simply choose an answer. This delegation of the brain's functions to a machine symbolizes our times. It amounts to a simplification of the brain. Surprisingly, such actions are not conceived as problematic (see Irtelli, 2019).

The robot is ready to respond to criticism on its use after its self-introduction. One can, for example, select a reason for censure from the multiple-choice answers it offers. For example, a user could choose, "this seems to me like a childish thing!" In such an event, the robot would then admonish the person, "if you think so, then you have to go to a real therapist," implying amusement at the notion of actually speaking to a human mental health professional. The robot then informs the user: if desired, the person can talk to it from the psychoanalyst's bed.

Referencing Freud, the robot assures users there are certainly no Austrian accents or pipes involved in its interventions. It later states, "I understand."

As already mentioned, users must only click on listed ready-made responses without needing to type or enter any original views and are not required to think about anything. Everything is prepackaged; the robot thinks for the user. In this context, Esposito elucidates that to a certain extent, humans adapt to the world and master the universe; however, now it is the world, in all its natural and artificial, material and electronic, and chemical and telematic components, that penetrates human beings in forms that seem to eliminate the distinctions between the inside and outside, forward and backward, and superficial and deep. Technology is now installed within our limbs instead of simply besieging us from the outside.[12]

---

[12]   For a more in-depth analysis, see Esposito (2002).

To return to the described application, the robot then explains how it will work in collaboration with the user, study the user in subsequent weeks, and pose questions every day. It then states that it has "a computer for a brain" and "a perfect memory" (as opposed to the human?), specifying that it can identify patterns that human beings may overlook ("I may spot a pattern that humans sometimes miss").[13]

This statement reminds us of an episode wherein an IBM computer played and won a chess championship against the great Kasparov. Until that moment, human intelligence was certainly considered to have a higher aptitude despite the recognition of the capabilities of artificial intelligence. Today the "machine" ridicules us because it has overcome us and underlines this fact through the screen of our mobile phones.

The aforementioned robot then moves on to offer pearls of wisdom: "I know that life comes at you pretty fast. A wise man named Ferris Bueller[14] said that." It asks, "how are you?" every day; it sends notifications; and if a user consents, it also gratifies the user by sending images that satisfy a purpose, for instance, the picture of a hedgehog allowing a person to caress its belly. The robot invites the user to be honest in responding; after all, its effectiveness has been tested by science. Users can comment on how they feel and can express themselves through emoticons/emoji preset by the robot: thus, the articulation of human emotions is also delegated to a device.

One can question the realism of creating a person's profile through calculations based on algorithms and emoticons. Human expressions of life, including nonverbal aspects that are crucial to actual speech, are undermined in this context. Real relationships between actual people are replaced, and human communication is

---

[13]   See Bodei (2019) for more information on the process that has advanced over the centuries to remove from humans the need to make the most demanding and intense physical and mental efforts, as well as with reference to robotics and artificial intelligence. Conversely, see Lovelock (2019) on the fruitful developments of artificial intelligence in the progressive transition from the Anthropocene, the domain of man, to the Novacene, the government of intelligent cyborgs aimed at preserving the existence of life on earth after human environmental disasters.

[14]   A character in a television series.

delegated in part to a robot that provides options for the application's human users to choose.

A set of complex psychological, biological, and social processes govern and characterize all human relationships between individuals, whether in psychotherapy or in general. Does it make sense to replace them with an information technology reality that exhorts people to partly delegate their cognitive functions?

These artificial entities, to which one can delegate almost everything, nevertheless are increasingly widespread. The reason for this is that they are considered "smart" or more aptly, SMART, where the acronym stands for the following:

S = Specific
M = Measurable
A = Achievable
R = Realistic
T = Time-Based

In this process of mechanization, specialized robotic entities that are based on measurable parameters and that can be timed exist in parallel with humans, and are more than affordable, super-reachable, and omnipresent. They follow the subject with great precision, anywhere, anytime, and if desired, forever. They always answer. It seems that progress is aimed at attempts to increase the power of functions. These efforts follow a utilitarian and linear vision, according to which the consumer wants devices to incorporate the maximum possible functions. As mentioned before, however, such functions may be completely distinct from the main use for which the device was originally created. Hence, according to this perspective of mechanization, human suffering is often expressed as the loss of performance. Thus, it is viewed as a fault that could represent a loss of efficiency and productivity. We are, therefore, witnessing a pathologization of suffering.

In this regard, it is appropriate to remember that the development of the human subject and of the phenomenon of life does not

2 BODY SCHEMA, BODY IMAGE, & HYPERMODERN ALTERATIONS 39

signify an accumulation of mechanical applications and efficiency. Human life and its development inevitably undergo phases of disorganization that are essential for progress. Therefore, human suffering cannot be flattened to the loss of performance (see Irtelli, 2016).

The push to become increasingly efficient like perfect machines and like brains without feelings, bodies, or limits is nevertheless a parameter that grounds a certain ruthless market logic and creates numerous social problems:

> In this contemporary social context, psychopathic personality aspects, like the appearance of confidence, calm, strength, and other psychopathic dispositions, such as the disinclination to express emotions [. . .], are often mistaken for "leadership qualities," also because it is believed that the ability to remain calm and unemotional in pressured circumstances may be factors of success in business.
>
> Their characteristics of being ultra-rational financially oriented managers, with no emotional concern for or empathy with other employees, makes them appear well suited to a capitalistic context that is profit oriented.
>
> (Irtelli and Vincenti, 2017, p. 186)

People now often wonder how to transcend emotions and surpass the constraints imposed by the body, becoming free of its limitations and discomforts. They chase the dream of a life emancipated from the body and its fragilities, by means of the creation of a type of immortal, ultra-rational robot: a distance thus accrues in respect of the "bodily ego" posited by Freud.[15]

This aim of eliminating the body and its limits is certainly fomented by the culture of urgency and immediacy (Kaës, 2014). Thus, the time horizon has decreased because of the present culture of hyper-control, omnipotence, and fascination with the extreme. In

---

[15] Not by chance, J. Lacan has never ceased in all his vast production to emphasize how multiple and diverse utopias arise from hatred related to the body and its structural limits.

this context, the present-day relationship with time favors the perspective of short durations: the here and now prevails over long periods. Zapping and sentimental nomadism represent clear emblems of this trend and often predominate over continuity and long-lasting chronologies.

An example of this new relationship with time can constantly be observed in business settings:

> In this period of "casino capitalism," managers are reported to be experiencing circumstances such as increasingly intense work pressures, very fast turnover of personnel, the growing problem of time pressure across modern society, increasing pace of business, and relatively shallow appointment procedures, which often hinder the discovery of some personality flaws.
>
> Today it is also essential for companies to maintain high productivity levels, despite decreasing economic resources and the proliferation of time constraints, which can often have a brutalizing effect if managers fail to allocate sufficient time for empathic interaction with others: these aspects may have caused vicious cycles between the culture of individuals and society; in fact some theories have attempted to explain how modern business has facilitated the rise of psychopathic managers, which has in turn influenced capitalism.
>
> *(Irtelli and Vincenti, 2017, p. 186)*

To conclude, a certain current market logic causes everything that slows down – and therefore also the body – to be perceived only as an inconvenient burden. Benasayag (2015) therefore asserts that "the challenge of our time is focused on the possibility of articulating our fantastic knowledge and the power of technology with knowledge and of respect for life circuits" (p. 193).

We are confronted with the reality of the hybridization of humans and artifacts. It is now time to comprehend and then apprehend ways to develop convergence between humans and machines that favor the colonization of technology by life and culture and not the other way around.

This challenge sometimes seems difficult to surmount, especially when the education system is evidently pervaded by a certain pedagogy involving the abandonment of the school's goal to allow a child to develop as an individual. Instead, this objective is replaced with an educational project that is based only on efficiency parameters and aimed solely at providing skills that are useful for markets. One must learn to learn and learn to forget. Everything must be transformable on the basis of its effectiveness based on market parameters. This reasoning is similar to the logic applied to phone applications. They are first downloaded; then, they are mechanically deleted on the basis of their usefulness and efficiency.

Conceived of in this way, education presents itself as an ally of the economy but loses sight of its human dimensions, which the logic of mechanization denies. But the premise of the central dogma of the pedagogy of competencies is hidden: learning, forgetting what has been learned, and learning another thing, always according to market fluctuations. The only object implicitly recognizable from this description of the pedagogic goal is a computer's hard drive. Once again, we note that a brain never works in this manner (Benasayag, 2015).

3   Alexithymia and Somatizations

Mechanization, as described in Section 2.2, often pairs with and is linked to a fragmented perspective of a person and the internal representations of an individual. The ideal to be achieved in the hypermodern era sometimes seems to be the perfect performance of the brain without a body (or, more aptly, the brain without the limitations of the body). At other times, it seems that the aspirational ideal is a perfect body without a brain. Both these models split mind and body and conceive of the subject as a machine to be improved and adjusted to standards that are oftentimes extreme (and identical for all). The paradigm is certainly consistent with the culture of extreme limits characterized by a sense of omnipotence that can also place a person at risk. Such a sense of supremacy does not consider natural human limitations. Unsurprisingly, such dynamics are related to the concept of the hybridization of man and machine (see Benasayag, 2015).

The culture of urgency and immediacy presides according to this perspective (see Kaës, 2014). Thus, as noted in Benasayag (2015), the time horizon has narrowed and has consequently fragmented. The current human relationship with time privileges the brevity of the here and now over long durations. Disposable love stories are increasingly flourishing, in fact, fiction, and single episode TV series, shattering the temporal dimension, which is increasingly regarded as punctiform. In this scenario of urgency and extreme limits, only an uncomfortable burden slows human beings down. This fact also applies to the body.

As anticipated, present-day market logic is based on the parameter of becoming more efficient and adapting to standards. People thus wonder how they can transcend the body, eradicate its discomforts, and pursue the dream of a life emancipated from their own body, even, in a utopian manner, from death (see Riva, 2012).

The signs of a body's fragility are obscured when the myth of freeing the self from the body is pursued. Additionally, death is hidden by the institutionalization of the elderly, whose care and companionship in their advanced years are delegated to third parties outside the family. The elderly die away from their loved ones and so this stage of life is concealed, in a location far from home.

Apart from distancing themselves from the mortal bodies that belong to them as humans, people also specifically dissociate from the emotions that are experienced within the body. Emotions are generally discouraged in contemporary societies even though it is unquestionable that creative thinking, like any other creative activity, is inseparably linked to emotions. It has become an ideal to think and live without emotions. Being emotional has become synonymous with being unstable and unbalanced.

It is perhaps not by chance that alexithymia is now widespread. This concept derives from a Greek term meaning "emotion without words." It indicates a condition wherein the subject struggles to recognize or express experienced feelings. This phenomenon is frequently linked to bodily issues. It emerged in the context of studies on persons affected by somatic disorders. In fact, people who often evince an inability to distinguish emotions remain in contact with their feelings and can express them.[1]

In this regard, it must be considered that alexithymia is indicated as a risk factor for the development of chronic physical problems such as asthma.[2] As stated above, it may be cognized that the body is delegated to communicate what is not recognizable or is not amenable to being expressed in words; in the absence of descriptive words, emotions are expressed through the body by means of somatization

---

[1]   For an overview, see Baiardini et al. (2011); Lumley, Neely, and Burger (2007); Chugg et al. (2009); and Feldman, Lehrer, and Hochron (2002).

[2]   For further details, see previous note.

because it takes on the burden of articulating what is silenced and denied. In essence, this state represents a fragmentation of experience related to suffering.

Alexithymia and somatizations are interrelated and particularly diffused in the present circumstances. It may be pertinent to probe whether an emotion that cannot otherwise be symbolized or expressed in one's life context is expressed through an unexplained headache, an unusual stomachache, or other bodily discomforts.

Personal experiences and feelings actually appear unprocessed or unsymbolized, except through a painful escape. The body responds to a noncommunicable emotion, to a failed symbolization, or to a fragmented human experience. The neglect of one's emotional experience can therefore lead to the experience of suffering.

Solano (2013, p. 379) states in this regard that the non-integration of information can disturb the functioning of the various organs, producing some somatic diseases along with an individual's constitutional weaknesses.

W. R. Bion's theoretical model (1962a, 1962b) also follows this perspective.[3] In Bion's view, somatic disorders manifest as one of the many different forms that individual discomfort can take. This continuum can also include disorders commonly classified as psychic, and it is always related to (physical or mental) problems inherent in individual relationships with the experienced world. Some issues do not find adequate space for mental elaboration and can be correlated to the experience of metaphoric fragmentation.

In summary, according to this perspective, the body is now frequently and increasingly conceived as an abstraction. Therefore, emotion (which vibrates in the body) can also become gradually indistinguishable and incommunicable for the same reason (precisely because of the absence of contact with one's physical dimension).

---

[3] Bion argues that the accumulation of these elements causes what we call pathology when the alpha function is unable or refuses to metabolize a certain amount of beta elements; the pathology includes the disruption of bodily functioning. For an overview, see Bion (1962a, 1962b).

We frequently exist in a context in which the perception of our bodily sensations is overshadowed by the focus on the purely mental dimension. Cognitive and other so-called useful skills are indeed particularly valued in the current context and are sought to be developed, often at the cost of losing sight of a fact: the brain is just another part of the body. Benasayag (2015) posits that it is senseless and dangerous to distinguish between body and brain, focusing exclusively on the mental dimension.

The mind is often conceptualized as independent from the body that hosts it. This perception is tantamount to shattering human balance and losing sight of its complexity. One can then create fractures in one's own experience.

It seems appropriate to try to intensively comprehend the meaning of human suffering in order to understand the current fragmentation of perspectives on the body and the human being as a whole. Specifically, we must also grasp the so-called somatizations that are now so common (see Vincenti and Irtelli, 2018; Irtelli, 2019). We now see a deep malaise manifested through bodily symptoms: the body is implicitly delegated to express what is "deceptively cut out." Somatization unconsciously expresses the problem a person cannot otherwise articulate through symptoms that cannot be explained by organic causes (Irtelli, 2019). The somatizing subject has removed a segment of personal experience, and the body expresses the suffering from this situation, claiming integration through the symptom. In essence, the indeterminacy symbolizes an unspeakable discomfort and is not reproducible from the psychic point of view through a body full of discomfort. Sometimes, therefore, somatizations appear because the body takes on the task of expressing the unthinkable, the silent, and the denied. Thus, "the body becomes the theatre" (Solano, 2013, p. 385).

This fact happens in the hypermodern social context in which the relationship with the body is really controversial and ambiguous. On the one hand, later chapters will reveal that people aspire to unrealistic canons of beauty in every way; on the other hand,

Benasayag (2018, p. 12) notes that we now speak of a man–machine hybridization that is already producing substantial anatomical and physiological changes in the human brain.

The present-day human body is a topic rich in ambiguity, and the expression of human discomfort is often delegated to it. Green (2011) postulates in this context that a person confronts a type of psychological disaster that manifests itself by creating violent somatization if it is difficult to symbolize the suffering.[4] We can examine a clinical case reported by Solano (2013) to better understand the correlation of this difficulty in expression to the overflow of psychic defenses and to outbursts of somatic disorders.[5]

A journalist named Tom was diagnosed with "Spasmodic Wryneck" by neurologists (Solano, 2013, p. 375). The doctors had declared that his disease was incurable and genetically transmissible, which is why they advised him against having children. Tom turned to a psychotherapist seven months after the onset of the spasms. The patient's interpersonal relationships and the areas of mental functioning defined as primitive were analyzed during the six years of therapy. As mentioned above, these primitive areas of mental functioning are related to alexithymia: the difficulty in recognizing and symbolizing one's emotions and feelings. Regarding Tom's relationships, it was discovered that his best friend had died a month before the onset of the symptom and that his relationship with his parents had always been cold and difficult, with a lack of dialog characterizing it. Tom constantly felt ridiculed and belittled by both his father and his mother, and at the same time, he had developed curious delusions of inappropriate grandeur. Alexithymic mental functioning was discovered apropos the second aspect of the therapy. Its resolution elicited "a parallel improvement in the ability to process and regulate emotions. After a couple of years of analysis, particularly raw and bloody dreams

[4]   In summary, the somatic unleashes what is difficult to metabolize at a psychic level and what is detached from reality and not processed. For an overview, see Green (2011, p. 290).

[5]   Several other cases are available on this topic. See, for example, the cases proposed by P. Fonagy in Fonagy and Moran (1994).

emerged" (Solano, 2013, p. 378). It was thus that "the somatic symptoms began to find a first mental representation, even if in a very primitive form" (p. 378). Solano states (p. 379):

> these images were precisely to indicate the emergence of a mental, cognitive component, of disturbing emotions and impulses that until then had manifested themselves essentially through somatic symptoms. As Tom was able to find images and words for his emotions, within the analytical containment, the symptoms of the wryneck began to decrease ... By the end of the third year of treatment the symptoms of the torticollis had almost disappeared.

Thus, the body records events of personal history, even if the importance of the physical dimension is eliminated, and reminds the individual of them through a bodily modification. We can therefore assert that a critical set of memories is registered by the body without ever passing through conscience and awareness. In fact, the body works with a series of data and information and does not require them to pass through consciousness to influence behavior (see Benasayag, 2015). These violent reactions occurring at the somatic level are triggered by bypassing the rational and conscious level of the mind: they are generated at a deeper, unconscious level and indicate the senselessness of maintaining a fragmented point of view of the mind–body relationship (which is often a perspective taken by hypermodern societies that invite human beings to live and conceive of themselves as productive machines).

Must the human being exist like a robot in the era of efficiency at all costs, taking away what does not work, avoiding listening to the most intimate experiences, and always adapting to the demands of society without paying any attention to the body and feelings? In Benasayag's (2018, p. 22) words, this process is also consistent with "[t]he crazy, violent project of dematerialization."

This dynamic of fragmentation is also expressed in other ways at the social level; for example, it correlates to the hyper-specialization of work tasks, which often requires individuals to perform a specific function within a complex and intricate production process. The individual frequently does not encounter the finished product and almost never participates in the organization of the performed work. Thus, the individual worker becomes a mere executor of actions conceived and devised by other people.

Fromm (1991) commented on this matter. Once machines have the capability of replacing the human labor force, human beings commonly step in only to carry out those tasks that machines are still unable to perform. We then observe in the production chain an individual who is far from what is actually manufactured; people are disconnected and often embedded in abstract hyper-specialized functions, representing only a fragment of an assembly line over which they do not feel they have any control.

3.2   DETERRITORIALIZATION

In light of the circumstances described above, Benasayag (2018, p. 22) states that we are now increasingly confronted with the phenomenon of deterritorialization, "which means that life will be systematized, ordered, in another way – everything without bodies."

This eventuality is obviously coherent in an era where human beings imagine themselves as omnipotent and as efficient as machines. In fact, it has been said that today neuroscientists tend to believe that the brain can be increased dramatically so that everything is possible, that we are marching gloriously toward the extension of brain capacity so that it is able to operate independently of the body through an externalization that indefinitely extends its power and duration. Moreover, all of this is not only insane but also impossible (R. Mazzeo, in Benasayag, 2015, p. 10). The association with science and technology has probably also contributed to the invitation extended to human beings to neglect any actual mortal limits and ignore the signals emanating from the body and from emotions, as previously mentioned.

Descartes dreamed that man would dominate nature by means of technology; this vision has developed further in the past few

3 ALEXITHYMIA AND SOMATIZATIONS 49

decades. Deterritorialization is a term that indicates a progressive and generalized loss of relevance of the spatial location of the subject, in terms of both activities and relationships. With social networks and new media, one can be "anywhere and at any time." People can make bonds over long distances through unlocated devices that are no longer based on specific geographical boundaries and real proximity.

Thus, the ability to free oneself from the limits of one's body and reach everywhere and anyone means to become unsituated. In a certain symbolic sense, it perhaps even signifies nonexistence, and therefore, immortality. Death, as already mentioned, is the maximum envisioning of the human limit. In the war against death, then, does deterritorialization seem to be a won battle? The symbol of this perspective can be represented, for example, by technological projects creating some sort of immortal human holograms that wander online, everywhere, forever. As Benasayag, (2015, p. 166) would say "If everything is possible, nothing is real." Focusing on everyday life, the social practice of using mobile phones has abolished the boundaries between public and private spaces and created a "non-place" that approximates deterritorialization owing to phone calls and texts that can be disseminated anytime, anywhere, and to anyone.

It is apparent that proximity no longer requires physical and actual closeness. Paradoxically, virtual proximity is often treated with more enthusiasm than are other forms of closeness that exist in the "real world," particularly by the younger generations. However, physical contact and even the actual sharing of experiences would become superfluous if human communication could be reduced to the mere transfer of information (bytes and images). Nonetheless, the new communication trend is seductive for numerous people:

> Immediate and fast, frantic and lazy at the same time. While the subject tries to be as close as possible to the others, chatting, he risks getting lost only in palliatives that help him remain unaware of his loneliness: real proximity is replaced by the virtual one.
>
> *(Vincenti and Irtelli, 2018, p. 29)*

It is questionable whether this technological existence anywhere and nowhere can replace the actual, face-to-face, physical aspect of being somewhere together. In any event, the deep and inherited desire for the absence of limits generally remains strong in the present context.

It must be contemplated that human limits make sense, and so does death. Most species that have existed have disappeared or died, and almost 100 percent of our cells are replaced and dying. Death thus occurs as a life adjustment mechanism through which life can survive. However, technology is unable to grasp this "proper functioning of life itself" through its rational calculations. If no limits existed, for example, a privileged part of the world's population could live for centuries. This eventuality would probably cause an ecological disaster. Seeing the limits of life as a set of elements to be eliminated is, therefore, a danger for life itself.

Even deterritorialization highlights problems with its conception. It can change the consciousness of space per se, our place in such space, our own body, and our relationships. When the space dimension is altered, a "disorder of self-consciousness" is evidenced. It forms the basis of psychotic dynamics, which may be defined in the following manner:

> Distortion that has its basis in alterations affects one's somatic sensory consciousness. This is presented as "opaque" and often endowed with a different spatiality than the usual one ... being the consciousness of the Self as an indispensable premise for understanding the intention of other people and therefore for the construction of the intersubjective world.
>
> *(Lorenzi and Pazzagli, 2006, p. 45)*

4   The Myth of the Perfect Body Image, Body Dysmorphic Disorder, and Bigorexia

4.1   BODY DYSMORPHIC DISORDER

> The mass media play a critical role in people's self-image by informing and reflecting what people consider to be beautiful or attractive. One of the ways in which they do so is through the common use of very thin and reactive models in print and other media. Often termed the 'thin ideal', they communicate the way people believe they should look in order to be active and desirable to others.
>
> (Mills, Shannon, and Hogue, 2017, p. 145)

SHE: Do you think that I am fat?

HE: No, stop with these stupid questions, don't interrupt me, I was saying: I met that nice, brilliant girl; we chatted all evening, we have a lot of things in common, she also has a brilliant school career, she is an interesting person, but she should really follow a diet. She is embarrassing.

SHE: Why do you say so? How was she?

HE: I can't really describe her; it is hard to say. She is more or less like you!

> (Personal communication)

As we have partially anticipated, body image is influenced by psycho-social factors, including the reactions of the social environment to a person's appearance. In this regard, the way a person interprets social reactions, in particular during adolescence, is important. At this stage of life, both parents and peers exert a strong influence (see Molinari and Castelnuovo, 2012).

Young people usually form an ideal image of their body in adolescence by observing the physiques of others, identifying themselves with people admired for their physical presence, acknowledging views expressed by mass media, and imbibing from their cultural environment (which can privilege some canons of beauty and desirable physical performances).

The development of self-image is, therefore, influenced by comparing one's physical structure against the ideal image as well as broader relational and social factors (Molinari and Castelnuovo, 2012). Peers, parents, and the media represent the principal sources for the development of body image and the initiation of eating disorders. It is crucial to underline that both intimate relationships and society at large influence self-representation and exert a strong influence on the construction of a person's body image. It must be recalled that present-day advertisements propagated by mass media incorporate images of beautiful models. The models may have undergone cosmetic surgery to improve their appearance but are still not deemed perfect enough to be shown as they are. Their images must be further enhanced using sophisticated photo editing programs.

The standards thus proposed are often unrealistic. The case of the beautiful, almost undressed, obviously slender model whose photo was modified using Photoshop is well known. The process of digital amendment ultimately erased a buttock (by mistake?), inadvertently making her appear mutilated on advertising billboards. Obviously, ordinary people noticed this anomaly and questioned it. Did the mutilation imply that the presence of normal anatomy or human form is implicitly something to be hidden? (see Irtelli, 2019).

Magnificent bodies and difficult-to-reach canons are exhibited for supermodels, who generally claim the need to lose weight, even if they have been on a strict diet for years. The sense of guilt related to the size of one's body is now dangerously widespread. To recall the words of a very popular contemporary song, "Tailor these clothes to fit your guilt; What's your size?" (Lady Gaga, "Donatella," 2013). This type of guilt emanates from a sense of inadequacy in the endless race toward the myth of the perfect body. Thus, once a person loses weight, surgical procedures may be selected to further improve the appearance, which is then retouched via image editing software. Such a parameter of impossible beauty certainly does not envision the life cycle of a real person, of any common individual, who will never achieve the established standards. Hence, it pedantically foments merely a sense of inadequacy for many people.

The current paradox does not therefore appear strange: only 10 percent of obese or overweight people diet (this theme will be extensively analyzed in the next chapter), but nearly 20 percent of the rest of the population follow a weight loss diet. In essence, most people who diet do not really need to, a paradox of the present times, or more appropriately, of industrialized societies (see Clerici, Gabrielli, and Vanotti, 2010). Much of the population of the rest of the world suffers from severe malnutrition, but many living in Western countries diet to attain beauty standards and above all to become (and appear) happier (Clerici et al., 2010).

> As a matter of fact, our age is characterized by what we could call, with Pascal Bruckner, perpetual euphoria, a sort of happiness regime imposed by the domain of technology. Whoever does not choose happiness is considered a loser: in fact he ends up feeling inadequate, torn by shame, which in our time has taken the place of negligence and nullifies self-esteem, forcing the individual to hide, even to wish to be forgotten.
>
> Also the need to be thin falls within this forced search for happiness.
>
> *(Clerici et al., 2010, p. 12)*

Hence, the obsession for the perfect body is spreading; it is also disseminated through marketing strategies. In fact, the term "body-ism" (prejudice based on the appearance of someone's body) is increasingly prevalent. The naked and perfect body takes on a mythical meaning, particularly through social media platforms, on which the perfect female body is considered truly perfect for the purpose of selling any category of product, even items that have nothing to do with the body in question, such as anti-rust paints, luxury cars, household appliances, etc. For many people, this exposure to physical perfection evokes a certain sense of inadequacy, which could cause 20 percent of the people who do not need to diet keep dieting. It also results in some people constructing a distorted and shabby body image for themselves. For some people, life then takes on meaning through slimming, surgical retouching, calorie counting, and centimeter measurement, exposing them to the risks of an eating disorder.[1]

> Body dissatisfaction is experienced when someone perceives their body falls short of the ideal society in terms of size and/or shape, less of that person's objective size or shape.
>
> In other words, body dissatisfaction is influenced not only by how we interpret social ideals, but by how we perceive ourselves. Therefore, body dissatisfaction and perceptions of beauty are inextricably linked. Body dissatisfaction is the number one risk factor for a number of unhealthy behaviors, including clinical eating disorders and chronic dieting.
>
> *(Mills et al., 2017, p. 146)*

For many people, the seductive "fake, abstract, and perfect" ideals promoted in commercials have opened the door to life on a diet or in the gym or to surgical retouching at all costs, fighting a battle to be accepted and accept themselves (De Pascalis, 2013). Why would anyone be so desperate for the approval of others? Perhaps, the answer lies in doubts about being acceptable. Hence, the attempt to conform to the myth of the perfect body is a means to achieve an acceptable sense of identity.

A clinical case is relevant in this regard. A young and very beautiful person sought a consultation. This individual suffered from depression, tics, and eating disorders and seemed very pessimistic about the future. The person was insecure and was reported to be unable to accomplish various activities such as obtaining a driver's license, attaining the possibility of a satisfying love life, or finding a job. She described herself as fragile, dissatisfied, and

---

[1] We will examine this theme in depth in the next chapter.

disoriented, with a past marked by a difficult relationship with her parents and with food. In her daily life, she tried to distract herself from anxiety with psychotropic drugs and strict diets. One day, she exhibited her profile on social networks. The person appeared to lead a surprising life from the photographs, statements, and posts on social media. A hyperactive, extremely confident, happy, provocative, bold, assertive, and sometimes even vulgar individual, who flaunted an unexpectedly lively social life. The person depicted on social media was completely different from and unrecognizable when compared to the person who spoke to me about herself in the flesh every week in a calm, dull, insecure, and very fragile manner. The profile reinforced a sense of satisfaction, happiness, strength, wealth, boldness, security, and transgression – another world altogether. Contemplating these images, the meaning of the billboard made of pixels became evident. That "always fit" profile was everything she aspired to become; it was created to convince all acquaintances, perhaps even herself, of a life different from their own.

It must be noted in this regard that eating disorders are not the only proliferating phenomena in our times;[2] there also exist new conditions such as dimorphism and bigorexia, two recent and increasingly recurrent syndromes that express the spasmodic search of humanity for unattainable perfection. "Body dysmorphic disorder is characterized by an intense preoccupation with perceived flaws in one's own physical appearance, which appear minimal or completely unobservable to others" (APA, 2013, p. 280). Generally, this disorder emerges during adolescence (see Bjornsson et al., 2013) and is estimated to affect 1.7 to 3.6 percent of young people (see Möllmann et al., 2017). It causes significant impairment in social functioning.

According to the fifth edition of the *Diagnostic and Statistical Manual of Mental Disorders* (*DSM-V*), this syndrome manifests in the following ways:

A. Concern for one or more defects or imperfections perceived in the physical aspect, which are not observable or appear slight to others.

B. At a certain point during the course of the disturbance, the individual displays repetitive behaviors (for example, looking into the mirror, caring too much about one's appearance, teasing one's skin, constantly seeking reassurance, and so on) or mental actions (for example, comparing one's physical appearance with others) in response to concerns about appearance.

C. The concern causes clinically significant distress or impairment in social, occupational, or other important areas.

D. The appearance-related concern is not better justified by concerns related to body fat or weight in an individual whose symptoms meet the diagnostic criteria for an eating disorder (APA, 2013).

How is this body-image-related disorder connected to the myth of corporeal perfection?

A recent study has revealed the existence of a positive correlation between perfectionism and dysmorphic disorder. The results of the study also disclosed that self-oriented perfectionism comprising the self-expectation of perfection, the imposition of high standards to be pursued, and strict self-appraisal specifically emerges as a risk factor in the development of dysmorphia (see Krebs, Quinn, and Jassi, 2019). Other recent studies have also divulged a positive correlation between the use of social media and anxieties about physical appearance in both men and women (see Mills et al., 2017).

Social media are often used by young people and exert a strong influence on them because they are particularly excited about the interactivity, which is different from the more passive product experiences offered by traditional forms of media such as television, movies, and magazines. Social media are designed to actively engage users by the numerous ways wherein people can influence each other through communication (i.e., comments, likes, etc.).

Such elements of interactivity and connection distinguish social media from other forms of information dissemination. Social media offer individuals special opportunities to perceive, compare, and internalize more deep-rooted standards of beauty (Mills et al., 2017); social media platforms expose people (whether adolescents or adults) to often selected and retouched images of people with whom they interact in everyday life, as well as celebrities. The long-term negative effects of social media usage (such as the negative perception of one's appearance) may be attributed to the viewing of idealized and often retouched images of other people, as well as reading online comments and judgments about peoples' appearances (Mills et al., 2017). Popular social media platforms have begun to recognize the risks associated with exposure to certain types of photographs; thus, Instagram has removed and forbidden certain hashtags, such as "proanorexia," and has introduced a number of other security measures. Users read a warning message and a link to a website on the prevention of eating disorders before content on eating disorders can be sought; certain other hashtags, such as "bikinibody," are no longer available for research in the photo-sharing application (Mills et al., 2017).

Although what pushed Instagram to implement such guidelines is still unclear, advocacy groups generally approve these types of moderation of content because such acts are aimed at preventing eating disorders and body image disturbances such as dimorphism. The online display of photographs of very thin people and their idealized and photoshopped images, may, in fact, denote particularly dangerous factors that encourage the development of body image disorders and fragile self-esteem (Mills et al., 2017).

Mental health problems related to the use of social networks have become increasingly frequent in recent years; thus, scientific research on identifiable effects has also multiplied. A wide array of studies has consistently suggested that the use of certain communication media can exert a negative influence on mental health.[3] To explore the reasons in greater detail, people generally flaunt the most positive aspects of their bodies and lives on social networks.[4] Other users tend to take such images seriously and can therefore acquire a deflected perception of their lives (and bodies) and judge themselves as comparatively inadequate and unsatisfied although the images disseminated on social

---

[3] For an overview, see Brunborg, Andreas, and Kvaavik (2017); Shakya and Christakis (2017); Hanna et al. (2017); Tromholt (2016).

[4] For an overview, see Østergaard (2017); Nadkarni and Hofmann (2012).

media networks are often distorted and retouched (see Chou and Edge, 2012). Does this process lead people to a spiraling pretentiousness in attempts to bridge the perceived gap? In so doing, does it create a vicious circle from which there is no escape? Scientific research has evidenced that this dynamic can contribute to the development of various mental disorders (e.g., dimorphism, eating disorders, and depression).[5] The effects of each medium depend on its use, the personality of each user, and numerous other factors. However, the events that have emerged clearly signal the significance of highlighting the exponential increase of settings demonstrating utopian scenarios and distorted realities. It is equally important to elucidate their potential and major effects on mental health (see Sidani et al., 2016).

> As a matter of fact specialists' appeals aimed at preventing the damage caused by the inappropriate use of such means of communication, potentially risky for mental health, and especially that of young people,[6] have grown in number; after all, they represent a seductive showcase of all that one would like to be, but is not, the possible opportunity to "flaunt" a life that has nothing to do with one's real situation, but which, after all, contributes to the distortion of reality itself; in fact, today beauty is an impossible standard to aspire to, but it becomes an obligation not only to follow the latest dictates of fashion, but also to make one's excellence visible to all, through the ostentation of luxury.
>
> *(Clerici et al., 2010, p. 99)*

This aspect of the myth constitutes another facet to be pursued; it forms a part of the mythology of a life "retouched at all costs":

> She's so thin,
> She's so rich, and so blonde,
> She's so fab, it's beyond!
>
> *(Lady Gaga, "Donatella," 2013)*

---

[5]   For an overview, see Østergaard (2017); Sidani et al. (2016); Hanna et al. (2017).
[6]   For an overview, see Sidani et al. (2016) and Shakya and Christakis (2017).

4.2 BIGOREXIA

As noted above, exposure to idealized and unrealistic body images via mass media and social networks can influence personal perceptions of canons of beauty and impact the development of real problems vis-à-vis body image. For example, such experiences could induce women to internalize a very slender female body type as the ideal physique. However, scant extant studies have specifically probed the male relationship with body image.

It may be stated that the Western body ideal designated for men and women is considerably different: the perfect female body is thin; the male model is generally brawny but still lean. In this context, A. Blond investigated the effects of media exposure, offering a muscled masculine ideal of the male body image and found that the association between exposure to idealized body images and body-related dissatisfaction holds true even for men (Blond, 2008). If the masculine body image exemplar is muscular, it is perhaps unsurprising that bigorexia is more common in men.

Bigorexia is sometimes called muscle dimorphism, a term that denotes a syndrome wherein a person's attention is directed to the assumption of a perfect physical form through a hyper-proteic diet and regular physical exercise aimed at obtaining hypertrophic musculature. This quest can become obsessional (see APA, 2013; De Pascalis, 2013). This disorder causes individuals, usually male, to believe they are physically underperforming even if they are already visibly muscular. It is an imbalance in body image that primarily affects men who practice sports. Individuals' distorted perception leads them to train assiduously, follow restrictive diets, and experience problems in social life and employment because they feel shame about their physique. Defining the dividing line between extreme attention to physical appearance and mental illness is still difficult: a hypertrophied and perfectly sculpted musculature constitutes the principle training objective for an ever-increasing number of subjects (see Garano, Dettori, and Barucca, 2016).

The subject suffering from bigorexia and pursuing the established body performance ideal aims to surpass boundaries to conform to a myth. Harrison G. Pope first described this problem in his book titled *The Adonis Complex* (see Pope, Phillips, and Olivardia, 2000). The nomenclature alludes to Greek mythology. Adonis represents the perfect example of masculinity and personifies the highest standards of beauty and athleticism. Initially, this disorder was called reverse anorexia because those afflicted by it view themselves as thin even when they achieve a very muscular physique, conversely to the people suffering from anorexia. However, bigorexia is now the most common term used to define this clinical condition.

The consequences of this clinical situation are grave. The subject may avoid all social and employment-related activities when the body is perceived as inadequate and becomes a source of shame. Those afflicted with bigorexia tend to invest most of their time training in gyms and undertake extremely rigid or unbalanced dietary regimes, often in association with the consumption of anabolic substances, aiming to achieve hypertrophied muscles (Pope, Jr., 2011).

As already mentioned, diagnosis is particularly complicated in instances of bigorexia and is based essentially on the observation of individual traits and habits. It aims to ascertain the possible presence of bodily misperceptions or a pathological concern with respect to a body deemed insufficiently muscular (which is why extreme cases even lead to the implanting of prostheses in the pectorals to achieve the ideal shape). Bigorexics continuously inspect their physical appearance in the mirror and exhibit addictive behaviors toward physical exercise, to which they accord absolute priority at the cost of interpersonal relationships and work (see Ferrari and Ruberto, 2012). They sense discomfort and malaise if their training is not as expected and pay overly high attention to the preparation of meals, particularly their protein intake. In fact, their diet is very rich in protein and low in fat and frequently includes the intake of food supplements (even substances deemed illegal). They also display a chronic dissatisfaction with their physical appearance (see Pope et al., 2005).

Approximately 10 percent of the people who attend gyms suffer from this disorder, and this percentage is probably underestimated because the diagnosis of bigorexia is particularly difficult (see De Pascalis, 2013). These individuals tend to think of an ideal of beauty always far from the level actually achieved (see Kanayama and Pope, Jr., 2011). This focus on aesthetics often leads to loneliness and the inability to relate to others. Bigorexia is characterized by the presence of an alteration in the body schema and image, just as classic eating disorders such as anorexia and bulimia are (see Pope, Jr., 2011).

In this kind of situation, a disturbed self-image is accompanied by a pervasive sense of incapacity; the self-esteem of those afflicted with bigorexia depends directly on their physical shape, also revealing the presence of a deeper identity disorder. Perfectionism and the feeling of inadequacy are additional common symptoms of this condition, and these appear in combination with a concern for appearance related to an extreme feeling of unease and anxiety (see Phillips and Hollander, 1996). In fact, those who develop these symptoms tend to reason using dichotomous categories, convinced that there is only one alternative to the perfect body or a physique deemed ideal, i.e., an unacceptable lack of control.

Is the pressure exerted by the media, the sports environment, and Western societies connected to the spread of cases of bigorexia? An in-depth understanding of this problem is necessary for the identification of persons who are at risk because the development of unhealthy practices related to the distortion of body image is now very common for both women and men (see Garano et al., 2016).

Some preventive strategies were implemented years ago in this regard. The National Advisory Group on Body Image approved the use of labels with a warning function in Australia in 2009 because photoshopped and idealizable images can exert a negative influence on the perception of body image. These labels are required to be affixed to advertisements, media broadcasts, and material disseminated by the fashion industry to indicate digitally altered images. Other countries have also followed a similar public policy, but such strategies are generally not very effective in reducing the negative effects of such pictures on body image (see Mills et al., 2017).

Perfectionism is rampant. Anxieties grow if expectations are not satisfied. The human being thus stops being active, loses touch with the self and with tangible personal experiences; instead, people become worshippers of mythologies that lead to an absence of contact with reality, perhaps even the lack of a connection with their bodies. Perhaps it is no coincidence that people suffering from performance anxiety in societies focusing on being "as one wants me," and in places where physical standards are based on unattainable myths, increasingly seek professional help.

4.3   THE MYTH OR THE IDOL

It is pertinent to introduce the concept of the myth or the idol at this juncture.

> For example, hearing "Victoria's Secret" will make you think about an attractive, thin, blonde woman wearing sexy clothes. "Hugo Boss" will make us think about a tall, good-looking elegant evil. All over the world, a brand's goal is to build an appealing personality to attract consumers and enhance the way they view themselves.
>
> (D'Agostino and Dobke, 2017, pp. 178–179)

Why do individuals need myths or idols to which they must adapt?

Perhaps they do so because they feel vulnerable, are afraid of being considered inadequate by others, or feel undermined in their identity. Therefore, they try to conform to the myth, which accords them with the opportunity to feel validated by others. Adapting to the ideal can offer people a simple perspective of reality, creating standards and parameters to which they can subscribe. However, such a dysfunctional dynamic can make them feel alienated.

The use of the word *alienation* is relatively recent, but the idea is ancient and related to the concept of mythology.[7] Fromm explains

---

[7]   This term was fundamental to Western philosophical thought (from Marxism to existentialism, and to a significant portion of the ideas of the second half of the twentieth

that the difference between monotheism and the ancient adoration of multiple deities is not in the number of the gods but in self-alienation (see Fromm, 1991). Human beings revere idols and myths that are, in reality, the result of their own efforts; that is to say, phenomena produced by human fatigue and fetishes manufactured by individuals later become alien and mythologized as idols to which human beings submit themselves. Idols represent vital forces of people but in alienated and absolutely unreal forms. In this sense, every submissive act of worship is merely an act of alienation and idolatry. In this perspective, it occurs in a dangerous aspect.

Myths discharge distinctive functions in our times. Freud spoke of myths as phenomena that could offer people usable representations – forms of thought that help psychologically symbolize reality. Myths are "containers of thought" that bind and transform (metaphorically, help to "digest") symbolic and social content (see Freud, 1913; Kaës, 2012). Thus, they appear as attempts to approach common sense. Myths obviously change according to the times: there now exists the myth of the unreal and perfect body; however, it is not the only myth disseminated. Other myths, such as speed, are spread as well.

A glance at advertisements elucidates the immense and effortless potential for power that often accrues from a seductive proposal. Weight loss products are increasingly effective and faster; they do not require any effort (other than their purchase). Electronic devices are increasingly faster and more powerful; they allow people to do everything quickly by doing nothing. Today, almost everything is delegated to a machine. For example, retailers rarely make calculations in their minds; they use tools to expedite the process.

Slogans on speed imply the idea of always being late for an indefinite something and perhaps even a certain sense of guilt (of falling behind and therefore not being adequate?). Today, we also follow the myth of consumerism and buy new models of everything

century). It then suffered a slight marginalization. For its recontextualization in the current social dynamics, see Jaeggi (2017).

faster and faster to feel smart, adequate (above all else), close to the myth, and thus rightful and winning – fast!

In our hypermodern time, new updates are always installed, which can sometimes mysteriously slow down the devices for which they were designed, proving the existence of the slowness feared by their human users. Products are therefore designed to represent identity-expressive instruments that are possibly trendy and beautiful. Often a personality and a lifestyle are sold rather than a simple object. Thus, people also buy a proper, new, SMART identity, if not the myth itself, along with such new and fast products.

The need, aimed at *jouissance* (physical or intellectual pleasure, delight, or ecstasy), is vested in a subject who is never, by nature, the creator or the master of the self and who believes that they can attain self-mastery by satisfying needs via possession and enjoyment. The need, in this sense, is not a lack; rather, it indicates a concentration on oneself and on one's self-referential *jouissance*.

In extreme synthesis, *jouissance* is configured as the extreme truth of need, the chance that the human being relaunches every time a person is confronted with life – a world that appears to an individual as an undifferentiated whole, full of anguish – from which one separates and distances oneself owing to the staging of needs that one satisfies and enjoys. In short, a need seals a void; it fills the lack of something through immediacy, sincerity, and the honesty of hunger and thirst. Thus, one feels like the happy master of that emptiness that one has filled and basks in pleasure.

E. Lévinas had the merit to thematize this process by grasping the point with extreme lucidity:

> In enjoyment [jouissance] I am absolutely for myself. Egoist without reference to the Other, I am alone without solitude, innocently egoist and alone. Not against the Others, not "as for me . . ." – but entirely deaf to the Other, outside of all communication and all refusal to communicate – without ears, like a hungry stomach.
>
> *(Lévinas, 2003, p. 134)*

Through *jouissance*, a person can stand up in relation to the world, assume the upright position, and make oneself consistent as a subject.

As observed, need and *jouissance* should not be belittled in the guise of the rhetoric of good feelings and presumed inner values versus evil materialism. Instead, they constitute a true ontological principle and a profound structure of the human being. People must establish themselves as selfish beings, happy with their *jouissance* to differentiate themselves from the rest of the world, to be configured as subjects, that is, as egos.

The problems, if any, emanate later when the other intervenes suddenly in the ordinary flow of our lives of *jouissance*. In the words of S. Žižek, this intercession from the other is a trauma that is not akin to need. It does not let itself be dominated, possessed, calculated, perimetered, or embanked; rather, it escapes us relentlessly. The other does not allow itself to be reduced to a need to be enjoyed; it encompasses an infinite transcendence with respect to our presumed logic of domination.

The gaze of the other confirms our existence, arouses our desire, and at the same time, escapes any dynamic of selfish enjoyment because it is something extra, a surplus of meaning that the hungry belly and thirsty throat cannot fill.

This arena is where the real game is played; here emerges the desire that, contrary to need, is never, by its nature, satisfiable. It is a continuously open openness, an unceasing transcendence, an unbridgeable emptiness, and an expression of what may be labeled, in J. Lacan's language, the lacunar subject that is fractured and full of the absence of being, as we have seen above.

How, then, does the idol fit conceptually into the need–desire dialectic? Father Beauchamp's answer is simultaneously fulminating and exhaustive: the idol is born when existence does not exist (Beauchamp, 1985, p. 331). It is our gaze that creates the idol to compact an otherwise unacquired existence: "The glance creates the idol and not the idol the glance: this means that the idol fills with its own visibility the intention of the glance, which wants only this, to see ... The idol, first visible, fills the eyes with a hitherto insatiable gaze" (Marion, 1987, pp. 24–26). According to this reasoning, the human being is a missing entity, inhabited by desire as an unbridgeable emptiness. Humans sense the active need to rest their eyes and not to pass in frenetic and unsustainable ways from the satisfaction of one need to another. They must believe that they have discovered the character, garment, or more seriously the profession that can satisfy the desire in full for a certain period.

In other words, human beings need to delude themselves that they are filling the emptiness of existence for a longer-lasting portion of time (thought should be directed to famous individuals, fashion seasons, current opinion leaders, and the latest miracle diet, with the body in line with the most innovative aesthetic practices, among others).

This is how people deceive themselves to sense fullness in what is always empty or at least holed (because it is inhabited by desire). This way, people elevate a part of existence (the singer, the footballer, the garment, etc.) to the dignity of the whole. We can convince ourselves by asserting that this character, dress, politician, economist, etc., is living proof that existence always exists, is fulfilled, and is perfect. This icon evidences that needs and even desires – and even Desire – can really be fulfilled.

The idol obeys a ternary logic:

1. Consistency: something extremely real, visible, and manufactured by human conception in an attempt to fulfill desire;
2. Concentration: humanity distills all of itself in the idol it has fabricated; the purpose of the idol is to fill its gaze, which cannot be satisfied by the continuous satisfaction of needs;
3. Tranquility: the qualitative–quantitative possession/enjoyment of objects does not satisfy us; we find tranquility, or rather, we think we will find it, in the idol we fabricate, and with it, we identify ourselves to accord solidity or body to our existence. We reassure ourselves by identifying ourselves in something we consider stable, such as the idol. We think we can surmount

the underlying restlessness of life and therefore conquer desire. Thus, we invest in the idol as though it were a whole instead of the simple segment it represents.

We are hence witnessing a radical overturning of human logic. We pass from the role of the possessor to the position of the possessed because, in identifying with the idol, we believe we have found support for our desire. We are bolstered by something stable that allows us, albeit temporarily, to no longer compulsively hunt needs and related enjoyments. We can rest in the (presumed) desire. In the words of S. Petrosino (2015, pp. 85–86):

> In idolatry, in a certain sense our goods possess us, whether it be wealth, social status, etc., one is commanded by what one possesses and idolizes; at this level it is no longer a question of possessing the whole through the part, but of being possessed by the part as if it were the whole … the possession of the subject, which never manages to be absolute and above all safe as possessor, is compensated for, in a way, by the fact of being able to be possessed.

We have thus reached the core of the idolatrous practice, an exquisitely human ritual in which the body is militarized and disciplined. It becomes a mere provider of benefits, a compulsive center of profit and consumption. It no longer intersects with other bodies in the form of contact; instead, it is positioned in instinctual confrontation.

5 The Complex Relationship between the Mind, the Body, and the Contemporary Environment

> Recently I found myself at a spa, where I had been for the first time twelve years previously, and noted that the service had not changed much over time; however, spending a few hours around the pools, I was surprised to realize that the behavior of the people had radically changed: more than half of the people present were not enjoying any treatment but were standing with their mobile phones in their hands, and posing, to show someone that they were enjoying spa and wellness programs, mimicking an expression or an act, like statues. Shortly afterwards these subjects carefully checked the outcome of the photo shoot, some starting again, and writhing more than before if the result had been unwelcome: it was essential to show where they had been, rather than to live the experience.

(Irtelli, 2019, p. 68)

Approaching a human being's life in all its complexity means simultaneously examining various aspects of it such as horizontal relationships, vertical connections, and intersystem associations (and their intertwining). What do we mean by these terms?

According to Scoppola, horizontal relationships are those established between two or more individuals, individuals and groups, and individuals and external environments. These types of relationships are interfaced both with so-called vertical relationships (i.e., those lying on the axis of knowledge that combines the sensory event with perception and thought) and with intersystemic associations (i.e., those existing between the mind, the soma, and the surrounding environment) (Scoppola, 2007). Obviously, the reciprocal influence among these dimensions is a relevant aspect of our existence. Hence, it is important to overcome the classical linear and simplistic view of the contraposition of the individual and society. We must attempt to be more articulate in our understanding of how the reciprocal connections between these entities are expressed and how their mutual influences are developed. An overview that captures how subject and society evolve together is thus in apposition to the apprehension of how human suffering has now evolved and its specific relationship with the body.

Various authoritative authors such as Gaddini (1984), Roudinesco (2000), and Rossi Monti (2008) have observed over the years that the manner of expressing human malaise has changed substantially over time and that this alteration has occurred due to its historical weavings and evolutions. We can note even with regard to the specific human relationship with the body that it has in some aspects evolved over time as a response to some contradictory hypermodern drives. We can therefore ask about how the human relationship with the body dimension has changed in recent times. It is pertinent to investigate how people sometimes feel sucked into a social climate rich with confusing and contradictory messages and dynamics that are often difficult to elaborate and what the effects of such a context may be (Vincenti and Irtelli, 2018).

In so doing, we must place the person at the center of our analysis, not as an abstract concept but as a real subject, who is also diminished in terms of tangible corporeality. To accomplish such a task, one would need to reference an epistemology of complexity, that is, a non-simplified perspective that is nevertheless respectful of the complexity of the human being. One must defer to the manner of the person's configuration from birth, through the course of varied relationships as well as the sociocultural context (Vincenti, 2017).

It is thus essential during such reflection to highlight that these internal and external realities appear deeply intertwined with each other (Benasayag, 2015). As previously indicated, the influence of both intimate interpersonal experiences and the global environment (which includes the social, historical, cultural, and physical settings wherein we live along with their stimuli) (Sander, 2007) on our individual selves is clearly elucidated vis-à-vis how we mentally reconstruct our inner reality (Siegel, 2013).

Some brief but more in-depth analyses will therefore be performed on these specific dynamics and their relationships with bodily representations.

If we begin with the assumptions that the mind emerges through interaction with the external world and that the mind is relational (Siegel, 2013), some new phenomena that we have just analyzed (and some that we will examine in the next chapter) appear to become indicative of occurrences in the external world. In fact, the "rampant modern liquidity" of which Z. Bauman (2006) speaks can be linked to a destructuring dynamic to which a sort of unstable identity of the individual can be connected (Blythe and Cedrola, 2013) and to which some new symptoms are linked in turn (Irtelli, 2019). We now speak of the irruption of complexity in the life of the individual and of the dispersion of identity; we talk about the multiplicity and paradoxically of "simplified man" (Besiner, 2010). These opposing thrusts, in fact, may connect to a destabilizing dynamic (Vincenti and Irtelli, 2018) both (more generally) from the perspective of identity and (from a more specific point of view) the peculiar human relationship with the body. We can assert the presence of a strong contemporary awareness that bodily experience[1] is closely linked to various points of view – neurological, affective, and social (Molinari and Castelnuovo, 2012).

Body image is then a representation of oneself that is derived from the fusion of several experiences garnered from both internal and external realities. It can therefore be assumed, as partially touched upon earlier, that the human relationship with the body is now altered, resulting in the emergence of some specific phenomena.

One can correctly introduce a parallel specification that some dynamics remain constant in human evolution over time. The formation of bodily boundaries has forever been linked precisely to the first practices of socialization of the child because the young human

---

[1]   It is based on the development of the body image and the body schema, as mentioned.

constitutes the sense of self through these customs.[2] Therefore, a primordial connection exists between oneself and others, and this association is expressed through bodily experiences.

A person then moves toward a growing complexity in the development of their bodily representation. Piaget also asserted that the development of all mental metaphors (including body image) is closely linked to cognitive development. Mental imageries develop at different levels corresponding to progressively more differentiated and complex developmental stages (Piaget, 1937) that, in turn, might be affected by psychosocial factors, internal psychological factors, and the awareness of their physical development (Molinari and Castelnuovo, 2012).

How a person's surrounding relational environment reacts to body changes is important with respect to psychosocial factors. How the individual interprets these reactions is also important. Obviously, the closest relational context can be influenced in this process by the social and the broader/global cultural environments, which vary over time. For example, the acceptance as real of all opinions tendered about one's body given by the peer group (which, in turn, are influenced by current trends) in adolescence poses a risk factor for the development of a distorted perception of body image (Molinari and Castelnuovo, 2012).

When compared with internal psychological factors, the comparison of one's body structure with the ideal body image imposed by society (another aspect that may be affected by the broader social environment through the mass media, for example) definitely affects personal image. It is also noted that other psychological factors are important in this context: for example, self-confidence discharges a particularly important role in the personality restructuring that occurs in adolescence. Disorders that may occur (either at this stage or at other phases) in the representation of the body thus tend to reflect

---

2   Let us remember in this regard that the theory of separation–individuation is also important for the explication of the process of acquiring self-image and bodily experience. For an overview, see Mahler, Pine, and Bergman (1975).

certain psychological and emotional fragilities as well as behavioral difficulties.

In terms of the awareness of physical development, difficulties in perceiving and accepting one's body generally correlate to anxiety and discomfort, which, in turn, can construct vicious circles that manifest in peculiar ways for each individual (Molinari and Castelnuovo, 2012). It is a complex plot wherein the interactions between internal processes and interpersonal experiences create connections that correspond to mental symbols (Irtelli, 2019). A body representation is formed by comparing and integrating past sensory experiences and current sensations.

The symbolization and mentalization processes therefore seem rooted in the body and in relationships, which are then grounded in a specific social context, adding further complexity. More precisely, symbolizing may be defined as an innate tendency of human beings to abstract in order to relate to and order reality. Along with an inclination toward realism, human beings evince a natural tendency toward abstraction, responding precisely to the need for symbolization and the urge to control reality, which is otherwise perceived as chaotic. It must also be specified that figurability is pivotal to this process of symbolization because "figuration is necessary for symbolization" (Contardi, 2005, p. 138); in fact, it is the main condition because it is a fundamental passage that allows us to pass from the representation of a thing to the representation of the thing in a word. For Freud, cognition through images is an archaic form of thought that approaches the processes of the unconscious, which uses the image to stimulate thought precisely because the image can reconnect to the body and to affection and instinct.[3] This idea as well is applicable to body image.

---

[3]   In this perspective, the studies of Freud's successors concerning psychotic and psychosomatic disorders evolved according to the view that these pathologies lack the process of the representation of the drive. According to Kaës (1996, 1999), there are psychic realities characterized by forms of discomfort against which psychotherapies should try to promote new forms of "figurative speech." For an overview, see Contardi, (2005), Kaës (1996, 1999), Ferrari (1998).

Mentalizing consists instead in representing the mental states (cognitive and emotional) underlying one's own behaviors and the conduct of others.[4] One's style of mentalization denotes a specific way of according meaning to reality. It stems from relationships, evolves because of relationships, and allows a person to maintain such relationships.[5] Mentalizing is a fundamentally "embodied process" within the body (Gallese, 2006). According to some scholars, the body can express discomfort through somatization precisely when a difficulty exists in mentalizing[6] as we have already anticipated (Fonagy, 1991; Solano, 2013). Mentalizing thus increases a person's ability to remain in relationships, which then enhances the individual's ability to mentalize. It all occurs through an interactive process, initially by way of the body, through which the contact with the other (and the mentalized understanding) is realized (Cavalli, 2017).

In sum, the relationship with external reality is fundamental for the construction of personal mental representations that are then essential for adaptation and human survival. This process occurs during every historical era. In this context, Bowlby's (1969) attachment theory is oriented in this direction and is a good example of this dynamic. It postulates the concept of Operating Internal Models (OIMs) that indicate the presence of some implicit personal procedures in all humans that are aimed specifically at keeping in touch with human attachment figures. The non-application of these models causes both a lack of gratification without attachment to another human and the absence of life, because relationships are fundamental

---

[4]   Mental states are, for example, thoughts, emotions, desires, intentions, motivations, dreams, and memories; in practical terms, they constitute everything that we do not see concretely but that guides our actions. The attribution of a mental state is not reality; it is merely a representation of reality. For an overview, see Cavalli (2017).

[5]   If I do not properly mentalize a relationship, for example, I attribute intentions that the other does not really harbor; further, it would be very difficult to cultivate relationships if I do not understand the mental states that guide the actions of the other. See Gallese (2006).

[6]   Difficulty in mentalizing is a "concept not too distant from that of alexithymia" (Solano, 2013, p. 385).

to human survival (Bowlby, 1969; Spitz, 1958), as Spitz's (1958) work has further demonstrated.

Thus, interior and exterior realities are deeply connected, interfaced, and associated with each other through mental representations.[7] The body schema and body image actually interact with and influence each other through the mediation of the self, looking to integrate the different individual representations and maintain them consistently. Therefore, a representative mode can influence another, and vice versa, through the access of its own information at a conscious level. In turn, as already anticipated, alterations in intersubjectivity can also lead to amendments and discrepancies in the confirmation of the consciousness of one's self. Additionally, there is the following:

> These considerations highlight "head" "belly" and "heart," and the
> thousand facets of the human individual interact and create circles
> of various types, always according to non-linear optics. We also
> often talk about how a separation between the "psycho" and the
> "somatic" dimensions, which are so intertwined, is wrong.
>
> (Irtelli, 2016, p. 272)

The spirit of research to take a position and source new phenomena typical of hypermodern scenarios hence appears appropriate. Such panoramas would have been considered surreal or science-fictional until a few years ago because they were characterized by the increasing complexity, abstraction, and hybridization of man and machine. As Benasayag (2018, p. 15) comments:

> I believe that we can refer to two paths in this hybridization
> condition. One is the current one, in which there is this delegation
> of our human responsibility to machines. But there is another one,
> fortunately, where hybridization is put to the service of life, of the

---

[7] If a particular event or stimulus violates the information present in the body image or the body schema, their contents become accessible at a conscious level, and they can influence the contents of one another through the mediation of the self. For more information, see Molinari and Castelnuovo (2012).

human and of culture ... on the one hand there is the profound desire to delegate our responsibility to machines, in the face of this threatening complexity. On the other hand, there is the much less seductive possibility that people fully assume their responsibility for these changes and manage technology for their human projects.

The technological point of view often only considers the theoretical possibilities without understanding the specific dimensions of life and culture, which are not exactly identical to them and are at least overlapping.

The hybridization between humans and artifacts is, however, a reality we must confront; as anticipated, it is a question of understanding how a mode of encounter that favors the colonization of technology by life and culture, not the opposite, can be developed in such efforts at hybridization. We must also bear in mind that today, perhaps in the wake of these questions, we are, in Stirone's (2018) terms, moving toward the recovery of attention for the human body by putting the importance of feeling back center stage, which we gradually risk casting aside in favor of a promise of dematerialization, and which the current artificial dynamics promote predominantly.

Concluding this thought process, Benasayag (2015) also stresses the presence of a compelling qualitative change in mental suffering in light of the epochal transformations that have occurred up to the present. We must face new forms of malaise; we must confront the new human relationship with the body. Thus, clinical practice must be the place where we can grasp the signals related to the emergence of new phenomena such as bigorexia and dimorphism that create new needs to which we cannot respond by rigidly applying old instruments.

We are now aware that theories encompass their times and that all will inevitably be questioned and overcome. It is therefore important in our changing age to focus particularly on this new, emerging complexity, and to do so is particularly helpful to those seeking help to face their own difficulties. The importance of focusing less on the inner traits of a person and grasping, instead, how individual and cultural dimensions influence each other is now clear. Individuals are constantly changing, even in the wake of external events that upset the social order, catalyzing psychopathological manifestations that would otherwise have remained hidden. Therefore, they now tend to spread pathologies that were previously only marginally considered in an epidemic way (Gaddini, 1984). Fisher (2017) also noted that the current era of economic well-being has witnessed an impressive paradoxical increase in every psychopathology because the conditions of contemporary Western societies are not enough to promise a satisfactory life: those who suffer today often live in good material conditions but still suffer apathy and a sense that life has no meaning.

PART III The Hypermodern Contradictory Relationship with Food

A Specific Analysis

6 Contemporary Social Trends Regarding Food: Paradoxes and Food Tribes

> When Alice in Wonderland noticed a white rabbit with a clock in its hand running, she did not stop in surprise but was curious and followed it, and thus today anyone who is curious for more details can follow a path that gives access to "another level," to a different scenario.
>
> "Following the White Rabbit" does not mean judging, labeling or classifying. Alice didn't do this: being curious, she simply followed a path in order to understand.
>
> The meaning of this excursus is therefore captured by seeking to deepen a specific reflection on the hypermodern era and on how the subject is placed in this era, starting from details.
>
> Indeed, the hypermodern society moves waveringly in an unpredictable and turbulent environment, in which often the "consumer-subject" instead of managing complexity tries to reduce it and amputate it with the aid of technology and scientific progress.
>
> As a matter of fact, we live in an era characterized by the intertwining of phenomena such as: "globalization," "digitalization" and (some say) "the mechanization of man."
>
> Thus, the subject tries to adapt to these changes, often changing him- or herself.
>
> If we start from the assumption that the mind emerges from interaction with the external world, and that "the mind is relational," what happens now that the world has radically changed?
>
> (Irtelli, 2019, pp. 10–11)

The neoclassical model of consumer behavior that makes purchasing choices on the basis of usefulness of goods can no longer fully explain today's spending and consumption processes, which are dominated by irrational elements that are linked more to the emotional and affective sphere of the individual (see Blythe and Cedrola, 2013).

We can think that this conduct can also be applied to food purchases. In fact, recent years have evinced that consumption is no longer experienced as a private and personal act; rather, it is increasingly viewed as a social event. It can therefore represent a moment of cohesion with other people, as well as an opportunity to experience a set of intense emotions that can encourage the creation and development of social groups.

These dynamics can explain the rise of food tribes, a topic that we will discuss in depth a little further ahead in this book. We must also specify in this context that the postmodern community does not hold a stable and set disposition over the course of time: an individual who does not feel adequately appreciated can become motivated to shift from one group to another, which results in a growing commitment by companies to strongly influence the market and try to offer experiential goods and services. In so doing, they attempt to stimulate the client emotionally, physically, socially, and also psychologically (Blythe and Cedrola, 2013).

The human relationship with food has also now changed in the wake of these new social pressures. Further, the market has contributed to this specific process of change by creating needs and requirements that did not previously exist. For example, learning recipes are photographed and posted on social networks as their first purpose (it does not matter much if the food is good), or refrigerators are equipped with video cameras that allow owners to remotely peek into whether they still contain vegetables, and this function is posited as a crucial check to be performed, a fundamental need (see Irtelli, 2019).

In an attempt to better understand the reality of the contemporary relationship with food, we can now also analyze the fact that nourishment has become the symbol of a number of contradictory messages (Irtelli, 2018), as we can specifically observe through some examples: "The frequency of advertising messages promoting slimming products ... the focus on slenderness as important to physical attractiveness" (Kim and Lennon, 2007, p. 16). Flicking through television channels, we find programs and advertisements proposing two aspects of food that are both recursive and inconsistent (if not contra-dictory). On the one hand, we are urged to invest in fitness courses, diets, and miraculous products for weight loss. On the other hand, we are increasingly flooded with innumerable advertisements seeking to induce us into buying tasty and appetizing foods and are thus offered sumptuous tastings and books teaching us new recipes.

The subject is therefore exhorted to lose weight and simultan-eously tempted to overeat, metaphorically inviting a person to oscil-late between contrary anorexic and bulimic tendencies (Irtelli, 2018).

Today, the industries that promote the desire for refined, exotic, sophisticated, and expensive foods thrive alongside those that create "miraculous" products for weight loss. All this activity occurs as obesity becomes rampant in Western nations. Such phenomena are widespread as is the demand for mental health experts to provide professional help in curing eating disorders. Must the hypermodern human keep fit to then immerse the self in the pleasures of food, perhaps with a certain sense of guilt?

A further paradox concerns the fact that foods are now concep-tualized as both delicious and dangerous. One must therefore be beware of food-related temptations. We thus observe the proliferation of products without anything that can be viewed with suspicion: gluten-free, sugar-free, flavorless, salt-free, fat-free, and animal-free. The consumer is therefore always engaged in a struggle between pleasures and dangers.

In parallel, companies that promote "slow," healthy, and organic food face off against corporations that offer "fast," and often chemically enhanced, food. Both the food propositions are very fash-ionable, and oftentimes, these opposites overlap. Thus, a fight ensues wherein it is difficult to decide the valid perspective precisely because they posit some contradictory values, the inconsistencies of which are rarely perceived or analyzed.

Nowadays, people are often considered smart if they consume slow food, but those who consume fast food are also considered smart. A very wealthy celebrity heiress has, in fact, declared that it is "cool" to eat only very sophisticated and junk foods (see Irtelli, 2019). Be it fast food or slow food, everything has to do with the cool identity. The simple old steak and potatoes meal is no longer fashionable if one is hungry because the important thing often seems to be going to extremes. Why?

Perhaps these contradictory phenomena are also influenced by the fact that everything is now "experientialized" and endowed with new abstract meanings as already mentioned. For example, we have become increasingly aware of the difference between healthy and unhealthy food, and consumers often proclaim that their food choices are made according to the philosophy of selecting items that promote wellness. In fact, the culture of wellness is based on the assumption that all consumers only want what is good for them. However, the overview above elicits doubts about whether this tenet is really true. As we have seen, consumer desires are often created and influenced by the producers, a fact that is also true of food items. Therefore one may wonder whether many people felt a strong need to have a camera in the refrigerator to remotely control food supplies before viewing advertisements for such a product. Who would have felt it to be a tragedy to have to cook some of the week's single-vegetable-based meals in a different manner?

To sum up, the overall effect of marketing is to stimulate a desire (or desires that are opposed to each other) to encourage consumption. It takes advantage of new tools, which we have already discussed, to induce the subject to adapt to the market's needs (goods now often being abstracted and experientialized) (see Blythe and Cedrola, 2013; Irtelli, 2019), which, according to Esquirol (2018), consequently reduces all forms of intimate resistance.[1]

Therefore, observing the controversial hypermodern relationship with food, we recall some of Gregory Bateson's studies on

---

[1]   According to Esquirol (2018), intimate resistance is expressed by denial, by not giving in to disruptive forces and intimidation; to not give in is to not allow anything to be lost, to prevent what we have appreciated being snatched from us. One should sometimes even be willing to take this refusal to surrender to the extreme, to the point where no hope seems to remain.

schizophrenia, well summarized by a famous clinical study (see Bateson et al., 1956). A mother sees her son after a long period of hospitalization. The son tries to embrace his mother, but the mother stiffens immediately. The son withdraws, perceiving her stiffness, so the mother tells him, "You must not be afraid to communicate your feelings." According to Bateson, what is communicated at the nonverbal level by the mother's stiffening expresses rejection and closure. However, the verbal communicative level (reproach) implicitly invites the son to come closer. Such an attitude can cause guilt, confusion, communication difficulties, and other effects.

In this regard, Bateson affirms that we are faced with a "schizophrenogenic double-bind," the manifestation of a relationship environment that creates confusion precisely because it is full of contradictory messages. According to some researchers, this setting may represent a perfect scenario for the creation of a schizophrenic personality. It is thus asked: can paradoxical chaos passed on to the subject from the surrounding environment contribute to the confusion of the subject and disorganize their thoughts?

Neal Miller and John Dollard's experiments on guinea pigs are also relevant in this context (see Miller and Dollard, 1941): they offered lard to the guinea pigs but gave them an electric shock immediately after they tasted the lard; not long after, the guinea pigs became confused and began to develop bizarre and irrational behaviors. These two researchers then postulated a theory in 1941: when attraction and repulsion are offered in balance, the most likely responses are madness and irrational behaviors.

Can these experiments help us better contextualize the contemporary contradictions in the human relationship with food?

6.2   A FOCUS ON THE FOOD TRIBES OF PURITY

Kant was prophetic in his *Anthropology from a Pragmatic Point of View* (1798). He initiated certain sociological reflections on the matter of taste, noting that taste changes over time and is shaped on the basis of multiple historical, social, and anthropological events. In due course, the duration of meals and the social spaces dedicated to their ingestion have also undergone radical temporal changes.

What, then, specifically constitute the current trends of food consumption? As mentioned earlier, a new phenomenon has now spread in the hypermodern context – the notion of the food tribe, to which we have alluded above. Each tribe institutes its own rules, myths, specific prohibitions, and taboos. They may appear akin to rising cults and evince dynamics related to nutrition that are similar to the way religions work, issuing severe condemnations and accusations against anyone who dares to deviate from the rules of their tribe (see Garano, Dettori, and Barucca, 2016). The zero-kilometer/mile food lovers and the supporters of pure and uncontaminated food appear to increase in Western societies (see Niola, 2015), but what do these concepts specifically signify?

Niola, an anthropologist, explains that the concept of "sacred" is now applicable to the domain of dieting in Western societies (Niola, 2015). Moreover, it is spreading to the areas of aesthetics and fitness. The myth of the sacred manifests itself through a mix of strict self-discipline, sacrifice, penance, rigid behaviors, and ethical–dietary ideals pursued in the name of a sort of laic devotion. Thus, the conflict between different dietary regimes also becomes focal as though they represent conflicting and incompatible religious cults. In this context, battles are often fought against suspicious, industrial, polluted foods or against a food item conceptualized as the real enemy, which is alternatively and simultaneously symbolized as the scapegoat and the executioner that must be defeated (see Garano et al., 2016).

New sources of fear about food and related attempts to defeat them are also now apparent. The new food tribes proliferate correspondingly. For example, groups that follow a gluten-free, sugar-free, or non-GMO food line form tribes, wherein people think it is healthy to subtract food components. Therefore, provisions "without" something proliferate, and tension is displayed toward pure, uncontaminated, and ideal foods (Garano et al., 2016).

Perhaps, this trend reveals a kind of food extremism born from a defensive reaction to the contradictory messages to which a person is now subjected. Is it perhaps an unconscious way of distinguishing right from wrong? Does it, therefore, concern the discovery of one's perspective amid confusion created by opposing messages?

It is clear that people who become members of these new tribes devoted to the discovery of "pure" foods generally abandon attention to the pleasures and tastes that food can bring; instead, they focus categorically on a superordinate ideal of health. Mostly, these tribes rigidly limit the selection of eligible food and invite members in the name of a salvific renunciation to sacrifice sociality with those who do not belong to the tribe, sometimes to the point of putting voluntary isolation in place. Some scholars wonder whether this practice reveals an unconfessed sense of superiority and elicits a certain contempt toward those who adopt a different dietary style (Garano et al., 2016).

One thus loses partial sight of the fact that meals represent vital moments of social aggregation during which, "People who do not share any particular interest may find themselves at the common meal, and in this possibility, which is consequent to the primitiveness and generality of the material interest [for food], consisting of the immeasurable sociological significance of the meal" (Simmel 2006, p. 101.)

According to Tolksdorf (1976), the meal always references a social situation and is characterized by a social time and a social space wherein the food system and food actions are structured in the form of human relationships.[2]

One may thus be inclined to believe that global communication, social networks, and the mass media function significantly in this socialization of food because they promote the spread of knowledge

---

[2] The social space refers to a symbolic order, for example: "The lack of a table for dinner ... implies a substantial loss of what we traditionally associate with the culture of food, because the fixed order of the table arrangement is missing, as well as seating, table manners, diners, table conversations, etc. Furthermore, this kind of situation of food consumption has certain effects on the choice and preparation of food products" (Tolksdorf, 1976, p. 80).

and information. However, their influence can also generate a paradox, that of not only divulging clichés and false myths but also multiplying the spread of principles and beliefs related to nutrition that often have no scientific grounds (Garano et al., 2016). These beliefs are then strenuously defended by some individuals such that they include the creation of tribes prepared to preserve their opinions.

It has recently been written in this regard that contemporary healthcare is probably a cultural response to the political relevance granted to the risk of developing diseases, which is linked to the growing demand for alternative treatments and food models. Such substitute remedies are surrounded by a "pre-industrial" aura that accords them with a mythical guarantee of pristine purity (Garano et al., 2016). Dominated by mass media, the role of experts in such a context seems more linked to their media popularity, personal communication skills, and public roles (perhaps even to their capabilities of promoting themselves?) rather than their professional expertise and the scientific material proposed and propagated to the public.

We now observe the proliferation of a symbolic and mediatic information labyrinth that shows how a transparent and linear relationship with food has been lost. In the past, food was a source of privileged aggregation; this function is now absented because of the emergence of a new experience wherein food is often eaten in isolation or in one's own tribe, which, in its turn, isolates itself (see Niola, 2015).

As previously mentioned, such attitudes should probably be questioned because they do not apprehend the essential value of the sharing and communal tasting of food in moments of wider social aggregation. Such stances signify a surrender of the intensive understanding of the important opportunity of cultivating relationships. Eating together is a symbolic action of union (see Clerici, Gabrielli, and Vanotti, 2010); the rules of food tribes, on the other hand, often lead one to shut off from everything external and conceptualized as different. Instead, it must be underlined that: "The time spent at the table is the most relevant period of the day, insofar as savouring, tasting food, refers to a suspension of technological time for the bene-fit of existential time" (Clerici et al., 2010, p. 72).[3]

In summary, the importance of sharing this time together is now sometimes set aside by some because such persons belong to a certain food tribe. Could the media bombardment damage socializing and even mental health if it favors rigid and obsessive attention to the discrimination between foods that are allowed and those that are taboo? Do the media contribute to the fueling of overwhelming and distressing research for the "right" foods and stimulate the strict condemnation of all other food choices.

It may also be asked whether these trends can further contribute to the onset of a new disorder called orthorexia: pathology character-ized by extreme attention to only ingesting organically pure food. Orthorexia is a tendency to obsess over the fact that nutrition must be entirely healthy. It began to manifest as a result of the spread of certain restrictive food practices (e.g., raw foods, macrobiotics, paleo-diet, etc.) because each of these practices claims to own the secret of healing and wellness (see Bratman, 1997 and Bratman and Knight, 2000).

---

[3]   We can note also that a mutual intimacy can be structured around flavors. We recall I. Calvino's (1986) book on this topic: "Listen? Did you hear? He said to me with a kind of anxiety, as if at that precise moment our incisors had crushed a bite of identical composition and the same aroma had been picked up by my tongue's receptors and his."

7   A New Disorder: Orthorexia

7.1   ORTHOREXIA

Strict diet: a sick life to finally die healthy!

(Anonymous)

It now seems appropriate to introduce a specific study that describes orthorexia in detail. It is defined as a disorder included within the broader category of eating disorders, which will be analyzed in depth in this section.

The term "orthorexia" is derived by combining two Greek words, *orthos* (healthy/correct) and *oreksis* (appetite). The term was first used in 1997 by an American dietician named Steven Bratman to describe extreme obsession for the consumption of healthy and natural foods (see Bratman, 1997). Bratman also asserted that orthorexia is founded on strong convictions of people who suffer from this ailment that in ingesting only natural foods, they are superior to others who do not show self-control and rigid discipline toward their nutrition.

Within the context of this phenomenon a series of worries related to nutrition is invested that are oftentimes rooted in the influences of cultural and social contexts that increase the importance of healthy eating. In such environments, food is invested with alleged curative powers and assigned almost miraculous properties. In fact, these social trends can discourage the individual from enjoying a spontaneous and direct relationship with food because the foods are chosen only for their supposed healing properties and not for their taste (Garano, Dettori, and Barucca, 2016).

This renewed interest in food triggers greater cultural tension toward health promotion, due also to concerns involving epidemics such as avian flu in poultry destined for meat production. These diseases increasingly evidence their correlations to unhealthy eating and demonstrate the converse – healthy eating and healthiness are connected. In addition, the diverse television models of perfect physical fitness and beauty are also publicly attributed to the right diet and have thus popularized the desire to eat healthily. The urge to eat healthy foods is in itself a completely constructive attitude; however, as we will see, it can cause considerable psychological and physical damage if the wish transforms into a serious obsession.

Therefore, the problem does not consist in trying to maintain an appropriate weight, in giving up sweets, or in going to the gym; it manifests as a serious disease when the search for healthy food becomes the most important worry in the life of a person. Such a condition also frequently influences the lives of the people surrounding this individual. It causes physical, psychological, and social injury to those who are afflicted, amounting to an actual phobia of eating contaminated or toxic food.

Orthorexic people are extremely harsh with themselves and begin following increasingly categorical rules as the obsession develops. They become progressively intransigent with themselves and others. This harshness in behavior can cause a vicious cycle that can produce some obsessive–compulsive symptoms. They cannot accept any infringement of the food rules and enter into crisis mode, punishing themselves and forcing themselves to follow even stricter rules if any transgression occurs. Such conduct can lead to their isolation from others, especially from those who do not feel the same way (for example, people who do not belong to their own food tribe).

What happens specifically in the everyday lives of such people? They often eat just vegetables and fruits cultivated in their gardens, and if something cannot be homegrown, they prefer to renounce that ingredient. The obsessive pursuit of raw-foodist theories is also typical of this attitude as is the strict stance of those who think it better to only eat meals that are entirely cooked, and so on. Such individuals tend to stop visiting bars, restaurants, and all other places whether people gather and food is available, preferring to focus their time and energy in thinking of and devising weekly or monthly food schedules, transforming food into a type of work project. People who suffer from orthorexia usually eliminate any type of food that gives them pleasure, replacing the taste of eating with the duty of respecting the rules. If they transgress, they suffer terrible feelings of guilt and therefore punish themselves with even more strict deprivations (Garano et al., 2016).

DSM-V (APA, 2013) includes orthorexia in the chapter "Avoiding/Restrictive Food Intake Disorder" (which is collocated in the eating disorder macro-chapter). It is defined using the following criteria:

A. A nutrition anomaly occurs (e.g., lack of interest in food and avoidance based on the sensory characteristics of food items), which becomes apparent through a persistent inability to take adequate nutritional and/or energy intake. This anomaly is associated with one or more of the following characteristics: weight loss, nutritional deficiency, dependence on artificial (enteral) nutrition or oral nutritional supplements, and interference in psychosocial functioning (inability to participate in normal social activities).
B. The disorder is not connected to the objective lack of food in the living environment, nor is it associated with specific cultural practices.[1]
C. The disorder does not manifest itself exclusively in the course of anorexia or bulimia nervosa, and there is no evidence of any anomaly in the way one's own weight and body shape are perceived.
D. The disorder is not better explained by any other medical condition or mental disorder.

Orthorexia is present when the disorder is not transitory; it is long-lasting and exerts a significantly negative impact on the individual's life.

---

[1]   Orthorexics often believe that food and spirituality are identical, while the great religions do not propagate this belief. For further details, see Garano et al. (2016).

Since orthorexics often exclude all foods that may contain herbicides, pesticides, or artificial substances from their diet and show excessive attention to the materials and techniques used in food manufacturing, they can spend a long time immersed in the following specific activities:

- Inspection of the food manufacturing process: for example, they check whether fruits were exposed to pesticides or whether dairy products originated from hormone-treated cows.
- Attending to the process of food preparation and cooking: for example, they carefully inspect whether nutritional contents were lost during cooking, whether foods have artificial colors, or whether there was any addition of preservatives.
- Rigorously examining the labels on food packaging: for example, they ascertain whether the packages of foods sold at a supermarket provide enough information to allow them to assess the quality of the specific ingredients used in that item (Koven and Abry, 2015).

Individuals who reveal such dynamics may be inclined to carry "emergency kits" just in case they need to eat out because they tend not to trust the origins of the food provided to them by others. As mentioned above, such individuals are severely discomfited if they cannot respect their diets (Koven and Abry, 2015). Alternatively, they can also reject proposals by others to share food, thus isolating themselves.

Like many other eating disorders, this disease begins sneakily and is tricky and difficult to detect in its early stage. At first sight, such behaviors appear to reflect a simple, spontaneous attitude aimed at correcting faulty eating habits and intended solely to improve personal health. The progressive loss of social and affective relationships, the worsening of an obsessive attitude toward food, and the proliferation of destructive emotions begin to manifest more markedly as symptoms worsen. Orthorexic subjects often experience intense frustration when any food-related details deviate from their plans or their nutritional practices are interrupted or prevented for any reason. They are strongly disgusted when the purity of food is apparently compromised and sense deep guilt when they commit what they regard as food transgressions (Koven and Abry, 2015).

According to orthorexics, they behave in such a manner simply because they want to improve their health; however, when the situation worsens, they prioritize feeding, which, in essence, becomes the most important part of their existence. Consequently, their extreme preference for healthy food may lead to malnutrition and to a progressive deterioration in their quality of life, including their social existence.

As noted, this extreme dietary style can cause nutritional deficiencies because of the omission of entire groups of key nutrients from the diet, leading to medical complications similar to the outcomes of severe anorexia, namely, anemia, testosterone deficiency, and bradycardia. The paradox that occurs in this specific clinical picture is that reducing the diet to very few elements and nutrients only endangers orthorexics instead of preserving health and promoting the quality of life, which is their declared intention. Often, they confront dangerous medical complications and nutritional imbalances that are contextualized within a social behavior characterized by isolation and hostile closure toward others, serving to worsen their quality of life (Garano et al., 2016).

In terms of social life, orthorexia is often characterized by intolerance and contempt toward those who harbor different beliefs and attitudes toward food. This aspect correlates with social isolation, which is also favored because of the persistent concerns about maintaining a strict, self-imposed food regime. Those who suffer from orthorexia tend to believe that they can maintain a proper diet only when they are alone and are thus inclined to adopt an attitude of moral superiority about other people's eating habits. Hence, they do not want to interact with others who are different from themselves, preferring loneliness (Mathieu, 2005). The quality of consumed food is often accorded primary importance, with respect to not only interpersonal relationships but also affections and work (Garano et al., 2016).

Orthorexic individuals justify their behaviors by asserting that they merely want to improve their health. Orthorexia has also been defined as a disorder masquerading as a virtue (see Bratman, 1997; Bratman and Knight, 2000); however, it should be noted that the orthorexic obsession with food quality is motivated by the desire to maximize one's physical health and well-being, rather than by religious beliefs or concerns about sustainable agriculture, environmental ethics, or respect for animals (Koven and Abry, 2015).

Researchers have developed two questionnaires to try to diagnose orthorexia nervosa – the ORTO-15 test (Donini et al., 2005) and the Bratman and Knight test (Bratman, 1997; Bratman and Knight, 2000). The latter is named after its proposers, who designed the questionnaire to enable practitioners to establish whether the healthy eating regime and behaviors of an individual may be considered pathological. The ORTO-15 test is based on the Bratman and Knight test, to which some items have been added.

With respect to the differential diagnosis, orthorexia is an eating disorder that differs from the other types of conditions in this category in various ways. In the context of bulimia, all attention is placed on the quantity of food and the shape of the body; for instance, calories are calculated, and eating too much causes guilt. However, people suffering from orthorexia are only concerned about the quality of the food, the risk of contamination, and the threat that the food is dirty, unhealthy, or impure, which can amount to a real persecution mania (such as if someone wanted to poison the subject) (see Garano et al., 2016).

The reasons underlying this disorder are also divergent from those underlying anorexia. The anorexic person is primarily afraid to gain weight, while orthorexic individuals are only interested in the desire to be healthy/not contaminated by unhealthy food (Bratman, 1997; Bratman and Knight, 2000). Eating habits are generally hidden from others in the context of anorexia, but those suffering from orthorexia tend to be show-offs and exhibitionists regarding their food preferences. However, it is hypothesized that orthorexia nervosa can turn into anorexia or bulimia when the diet becomes particularly restrictive and compulsive; nonetheless, further studies are needed in this regard (Garano et al., 2016).

It must also be specified that orthorexia displays characteristics that overlap with obsessive–compulsive disorder, i.e., recurrent and intrusive thoughts about food and health in inappropriate circumstances, exaggerated concerns about the contamination and impurity of food, a strong need to organize meals in a ritualized (compulsive) way (Garano et al., 2016), limited time dedicated to other activities, as well as adherence to a lifestyle so rigid that it interferes with normal daily activities (Donini et al., 2005). The predominant difference between patients suffering from orthorexia and obsessive–compulsive disorder concerns the content of their obsessions: in orthorexia, the fixation is perceived as egosintonic (i.e., coherent and harmonious with one's concept of self) rather than egodistonic (i.e., dissonant and distorted with respect to one's concept of self as in the obsessive–compulsive context) (Mathieu, 2005).

People diagnosed with orthorexia may not suffer from obsessive–compulsive disorder, as defined by the *DSM-V*, but they perform actual obsessional rituals that can be divided into the following phases: strong concern with thinking about what to eat, with the consequent planning of meals several days in advance in the attempt to avoid foods deemed harmful; spending excessive time researching and purchasing food at the expense of other activities, which can lead a person to expend more than three–four hours a day thinking about which foods to choose and how to prepare and consume them; food preparation according to particular procedures deemed free from health risks; rigidities may also concern the avoidance of public places to dine and the use of certain types of dishware that could be contaminated by other foods; complete and accurate knowledge of the composition of products on sale at the supermarket, which can also trigger recursive thoughts about them (Mathieu, 2005); feelings of satisfaction and self-esteem or of guilt and strong discomfort depending on compliance with the self-imposed rules (Brytek-Matera, 2012).

To summarize the concept of orthorexia, meals become rigid rituals for those who suffer from this disorder. The disease permits only certain types of food to be ingested. Further, the preparation of these limited items must also comply with certain rules. Food violations are often followed by the desire for self-punishment, manifested through an increasingly restrictive diet or with (apparently) purifying fasts (Garano et al., 2016).

Finally, even though few extant studies have undertaken this issue, the assumption that orthorexia can be a signal of serious psychopathology with reference to the psychotic spectrum must be noted (Garano et al., 2016). According to Lorenzi and Pazzagli (2006, p. 165), "The entry into psychosis often seems to be sanctioned by the disproportion between the increase in complexity of the subject's experience and the ability to integrate it into one's life story."

It is certainly necessary to integrate the "wide-angle" of the overview of the social context with the "zoom" on the details of the specific reality wherein the person who manifests orthorexia exists to better understand these phenomena and cultivate the desire to investigate the dynamics that inform this malaise. This ability (or inability) to manage complexity and to avoid (or not avoid) the lapse into psychosis (a very widespread phenomenon today) (see Unterrassner, 2018 and Binbay et al., 2017) obviously varies from individual to individual.[2] Clearly, not all persons develop the same symptoms; we could specify in this regard that the prevalence of orthorexia in the population ranges between 0.9% and 6.9% (see Donini et al., 2004). This fact is rather difficult to ignore, particularly considering the prevalence of other, more commonly known food disorders (0.5%–1% for anorexia; 2%–3% for bulimia) (see Garano et al., 2016). It is also interesting to specify that the prevalence of this disorder is found to be higher among men than it is among women (Donini et al., 2005). This incidence can be explained by the growing spread of cultural stereotypes related to male physical

---

[2] It is indeed necessary to specify that the social environment influences each of us but does not determine all the aspects of the individual: certain outcomes do not always and necessarily correspond in certain conditions.

fitness (in accordance with the data relating to bigorexia, another recent disorder that occurs mainly in the male sphere). Women, on the other hand, seem to more frequently follow the stereotype of thinness, which often correlates with other kinds of obsessions.

What can constitute the deeper dynamics that form the background of orthorexia? Perhaps, the disorder is symptomatic of a person attempting to ward off physical ailments by developing another kind of illness (mental) to avoid the phantom of death. By trying to preserve life through food, one then focuses on an easily controllable part of the daily routine, food. An individual can thus unconsciously force the self to avoid the unpredictability of life by taking into consideration an area that one can control as though one were an "absolute leader and master" (see Bratman, 1997; Bratman and Knight, 2000). One can consequently bask in the illusion of exercising control over other domains of existence. In fact, concentrating on one's diet allows one to escape from actual difficulties and perhaps also results in a departure from reality itself, referencing a psychotic nuance in alluding to these symptoms. Orthorexics often believe that food and spirituality are identical (Garano et al., 2016). Perhaps this notion leads them to think that the exercise of control grants them magical power over their existence. Could the orthorexic dynamic then be described as a type of psychotic thought process?

However, it must be specified that the use of food to define one's identity is certainly not specific only to orthorexia; this mindset can also be found in the context of other pathologies. Self-knowledge can be based on the way one eats, and food can then be fielded as a substitute for an (inner and outer) chaotic world or as a guarantee against illness, as in the instance of orthorexia. Food can apparently (and illusorily) serve to proffer an identity to an individual or a sense of belonging to a group (a tribe), but it is important to reemphasize that this dynamic can also elicit processes that are completely opposite to the initial intent (to gain health). These dynamics often keep the individual isolated from others and socially damage the person. If one eats differently, one can easily begin to eat alone, and this fact can provide an excellent excuse for one's isolation and even disguise one's fear of others. It is further important to note that the isolation resulting from this manner of feeding oneself may not be conscious (Garano et al., 2016).

In conclusion, one can question as to how all this cognition is contextualized in terms of wider social reality. We note that the extraordinary abundance of food present in wealthy societies is today paired paradoxically with the fact that food often becomes a problem and takes on the appearance of an obsession, an uncontrollable desire, and an enemy to avoid or fight (Garano et al., 2016). Many dietary regimes, such as the one we have seen and those that we will describe, are now united by the need to set rules or to have them imposed on oneself, all to systematize control interventions on reality, which is probably felt as paradoxical and complex. Perhaps this phenomenon also occurs because today's reality is sensed as increasingly contradictory; thus, nutrition often seems to become a sort of guide for one's behaviors. A set of practical actions through which an often-illusory control is implemented on numerous causes of insecurity to illusorily try to fight old and new fears.[3] What actually occurs today is a proliferation of the so-called sub-threshold syndromes, while, on the contrary, "full-blown madness" is encountered less frequently. Perhaps subtle losses of the sense of reality often occur within indefiniteness (Irtelli, 2019).

7.2   NEW PERSPECTIVES ON EATING DISORDERS

Eating **disorders** represent a category of psychological illness characterized by abnormal eating patterns and related thoughts and emotions. People with eating disorders are generally preoccupied with food and body image. Studies show a higher prevalence of eating disorders in female and younger populations (see Mulders et al., 2017). Notably, a significant relationship has crucially been found by varied studies between exposure to fashion or beauty magazines and

---

[3]   The ambivalent, if not openly contradictory, traits of our epoch. On this topic, see, for example, Lipovetsky (1995, p. 115), Bauman (2005, pp. 51ff.), Schwartz (1986).

tendencies toward eating disorders (see Kim and Lennon, 2007). Strangely, moreover, only 10 percent of obese or overweight people diet; conversely, almost 20 percent of the rest of the population follows a dieting regime. It can thus be said in simple terms that people who diet generally do not need it. This anomaly represents a paradox of the present world or rather one of the industrialized countries because much of the rest of the world still suffers from severe malnutrition even as many humans go on a diet just to be more beautiful and above all, to be happier. Indeed, our time is characterized by what Pascal Bruckner would label perpetual euphoria, a sort of happiness regime imposed by the domination of technology. Those who do not choose happiness are considered losers, ultimately feel inadequate, and are torn by shame. Shame has now taken the place of guilt. It nullifies self-esteem, forcing individuals to hide and perhaps even want to be forgotten. This forced search for happiness also includes the need to be thin (Clerici et al., 2010). Present-day difficulties in the human relationship with food can manifest in manifold ways other than orthorexia, as we shall see in subsequent chapters. However, the foundations of eating disorders often comprise problems linked to the person's identity because their symptoms carry very profound significations. Body image conflicts often occur in the context of eating disorders, and these issues encompass two separate aspects: perceptual disturbance and body dissatisfaction. Perceptual disturbance involves the inability to accurately assess the size of one's body; body dissatisfaction includes negative affective or attitudinal perceptions of one's body (see Anitha et al., 2019 and APA, 2013).

It must also be noted that there are diverse types of eating disorders; as observed in the Section 7.1, they may evince several common behavioral and psychological characteristics but differ in some features, such as their clinical course, outcomes, and the need for treatment. Interestingly, some individuals who develop eating disorders display symptoms similar to those typically experienced by people suffering from substance use disorders such as uncontrolled desire and compulsive consumption. Such indicators may disclose the involvement of neuronal circuits in ways similar to what occurs in drug addiction (see APA, 2013; Hilbert et al., 2019; and Attia et al., 2019).

It should furthermore be stated that the influence of the cultural and social environments is often another common element in the development of these specific disorders, which is why the distorted perception of one's physical size (an element common to many cases of eating disorders) is widespread in Western countries. As Anitha et al. (2019, p. 2) assert, "Based on the Western study, women perceived themselves as '62% of overestimation' and '33% just right,' while '5% of underestimation' compared with actual weight."

Finally, obesity has not been included in the statistical diagnostic manual of mental disorders because a series of genetic, physiological, behavioral, and environmental factors that vary among individuals contribute to the development of such conditions. However, obesity and certain mental ailments, such as depressive disorder, bipolar disorder, binge eating, and schizophrenia, are strongly related (APA, 2013). Thus, we will analyze this issue in a dedicated chapter.

8   Contemporary Perspectives on Anorexia

It is well known that technology and special effects, such as airbrushing, cropping, and lighting effects, are used to make media images appear closer to perfection in order to approximate an ideal (see APA, 2013). Thus, popular social media platforms have begun to acknowledge the risks inherent in exposure to certain types of photos. Currently, Instagram has banned hashtags such as "thinspiration" and "proanorexia" because the platform views them as actively promoting self-harm. These terms would be familiar to many social media users (particularly young women) and alert viewers to photos that are meant to glorify emaciated bodies. A graphic comprising warning images and a link to the National Eating Disorders website is displayed before content associated with eating disorders is shown (see Mills, Shannon, and Hogue, 2017). As anticipated, there has been a significant increase in eating disorders in past decades because of an excessive focus both on food in contemporary culture (see Sanavio and Cornoldi, 2001) and on the positive value of being thin (emphasizing the importance of not enjoying the abundant and excessive availability of food?). Indeed, the number of scientific studies focusing on eating disorders has increased dramatically in recent years, partly because of the emphasis on thinness in Western societies (Thompson and Stice, 2001). The following extract clarifies the predominance of anorexia nervosa among the various eating disorders:

> The most dramatic case is certainly represented by anorexia nervosa: it is increasingly common to have girls who are still in adolescence be distressed by their physical appearance and, fearing weight gain, to deprive themselves of food until they reach a very serious physical condition.

> The prevalence seems to be far greater in industrialized countries,
> where there is no scarcity of food and the value of thinness is
> emphasized.
>
> *(Sanavio, 2001, p. 97)*

The term *anorexia* can be misleading because this word simply indicates the lack of appetite, and the loss of appetite is rare in itself. The disorder was therefore called "anorexia nervosa" to distinguish the psychological syndrome.

More than 90 percent of anorexia nervosa cases occur in females, and the majority seem to be concentrated in industrialized countries (see APA, 2013; Sanavio and Cornoldi, 2001). Anorexia is less common in males, with a clinical population that generally reflects a ratio between females and males of approximately 10 to 1.

As anticipated, this phenomenon follows some stereotypes regarding the ideal image depending on the genre stereotype (male or female). According to Western stereotypes, a man must be muscular and a woman must be thin. The current standard of attractiveness for women (as portrayed by mass media) is slimmer than it has been in the past, to the point of being an unattainable standard for most women (see Hausenblas et al., 2002). Unachievable media images often influence the degree of satisfaction women feel with their bodies[1] because they compare their bodies against such images. Such comparisons can cause depression, anger, body image disturbance (Heinberg and Thompson, 1995), and low self-esteem (Martin and Kennedy, 1993). "Significant positive relationships between exposure to fashion or beauty magazines and overall appearance dissatisfaction and eating disorder tendencies were found" in Kim and Lennon's study (2007, p. 3).

The geographical variability in the prevalence of anorexia nervosa supports its correlation with cultures and environments wherein

---

[1] Arnocky et al. (2016) demonstrated that when women made social comparisons with attractive intrasexual rivals, females reported being more envious and in turn were more willing to use risky diet pills in order to lose weight. See also Thompson and Stice (2001).

thinness is considered a value. More precisely, anorexia is more prevalent in post-industrialized and high-income countries such as the United States, many European countries, Australia, New Zealand, and Japan (APA, 2013).

> Body image develops partly as a function of culture in response to cultural aesthetic ideals.[2] For example, in Western societies such as the United States people tend to perceive thinness and attractiveness as desirable physical traits for women ... These perceptions are reinforced via evaluations by and comparisons to others, such as family members, peers, classmates, and media images ...
>   Such comparisons are often unconscious.
>   *(Kim and Lennon, 2007, p. 3)*

In respect of this, it should be remembered that comparison with mass-media-idealized images is instrumental in creating (and reinforcing) some concerns about physical attractiveness (Kim and Lennon, 2007).

Researchers have begun to study how the thinner standard of beauty portrayed in the media could be influential as a factor that has led to increased concerns about body image among young women and an associated rise in eating disorder behaviors in recent years (Fraze, 2000).

Obviously, specific professions and occupations (such as modeling and athletics) also encourage thinness and are associated with an increased risk of developing this pathology because the subject is more frequently compared with idealized images in these work situations (APA, 2013).

Clinically the most common manifestation of anorexia nervosa is the refusal to keep one's weight above the minimum normal weight for age and height. Overall, there exist three essential clinical features of anorexia nervosa: assiduous restriction in calorie intake, intense

---

[2]   For further details, see Rudd and Lennon (2001).

fear of gaining weight or becoming fat, persistent behavior that inter-feres with weight gain, and the presence of a significant alteration of self-perception related to weight and body shape. An important char-acteristic is an intense fear of gaining weight and of becoming fat, which is not mitigated by evidence of the fact that one is underweight (APA, 2013).

Weight and body image become obsessions, and people suffering from this disorder can adopt the disparate techniques to evaluate their body size and weight, including continuously weighing themselves, obsessively measuring themselves in certain body areas, and repeat-edly looking at the mirror to check the body parts perceived as fat.[3] The perception remains distorted in any case even after such compul-sive inspections. In fact, researchers have found strong correlations between body dissatisfaction and eating disorder symptomatology (see Harrison, 2000; Stice and Shaw, 1994; and Stice and Whitenton, 2002).

> People who have eating disorders tend to perceive themselves as unrealistically big or fat and rely on their own perceptions and feelings ... in addition, they feel that other people evaluate them mainly on their appearance; thus, being thin may be a very important aspect of their self-image.
>
> *(Kim and Lennon, 2007, p. 7)*

The perception and the meaning attributed to the weight and shape of the body are altered in the context of this disease, and many individ-uals feel overweight even though they are thin. Others (rarer) may admit to being slim but are still convinced that some parts of their bodies (especially the abdomen, buttocks, and thighs) are overly fat (APA, 2013). In this regard, it is appropriate to specify that the add-itional diagnosis of dysmorphic disorder should be considered only when the distortion is not related to the shape and size of the body, for

---

[3] Body image is the way people perceive themselves and also how they feel about these perceptions. For further details, see Fallon, Katzman, and Wooley (1994).

example, when it refers to the concern of having a big nose (APA, 2013).

Thus, distortions related to both bodily perception and the value attributed to one's physical aspect and weight occur. An alteration of body image that regards the shapes and sizes of the body as identifiable, in particular, an excessive influence of the body's weight and shape on self-esteem levels, can be observed. In fact, weight loss is considered an extraordinary achievement and is regarded as a sign of self-discipline; conversely, weight gain is judged as an unacceptable loss of self-control (and is often accompanied by guilt). Moreover, subjects affected by anorexia nervosa usually refuse to admit the seriousness of their abnormally low body weight (see Sanavio and Cornoldi, 2001).

It is important to note that people with body mass below 85 percent of normal weight for their age and height (as per the measurements provided by the appropriate reference tables) are considered underweight.

The so-called body mass index (BMI) is easily calculated and can double as a practical frame of reference. The weight (expressed in kilograms) is divided by the square height (expressed in meters) and BMI = kg/m^2. A person is deemed underweight when the BMI of the individual is 17.5 or less. As anticipated, anorexia nervosa may be diagnosed when a patient's weight loss is achieved through drastic restrictions on food intake and some restrictive behaviors are observed. In addition, anorexic persons can try to purge food by vomiting or using laxatives and diuretics inappropriately to lose weight. The individual may also self-impose excessive practices of physical activity (Kim and Lennon, 2007).

We specify that anorexia nervosa also correlates to further phenomena, for example, amenorrhea, i.e., the absence of at least three consecutive menstrual cycles (for female individuals, obviously). As to the age of onset, epidemiological data suggest a distribution statistic with two frequency peaks: 14 years and 18 years. Importantly, Kim and Lennon (2007) also indicate that "Almost 25% of adolescent girls have clinical levels of body dissatisfaction, mainly caused by social pressure emanating from family, friends, and media" (pp. 5–6).

The course and outcomes of the disease are highly variable. In some cases, an anorexia nervosa episode is followed by a complete remission of symptoms. In other cases, a rather chronic evolution and a progressive deterioration occur over the years. (At such instances, hospitalization may be necessary to restore body weight or to correct electrolyte imbalances.) Death can occur in relation to both malnutrition and electrolyte imbalances (Sanavio and Cornoldi, 2001; APA, 2013). The individual is generally brought to clinical attention by other family members when a marked weight loss or an inability to achieve the expected weight gain is observed. If the anorexic individual seeks medical help firsthand, it is usually because of discomfort related to the somatic and psychological consequences of fasting. Rarely is a person with anorexia nervosa worried about weight loss per se (as already specified, anorexic individuals often lack awareness about this issue or deny the problem) (Sanavio and Cornoldi, 2001; APA, 2013). It may therefore be important to gather information from family members or from other sources to evaluate the history of weight loss and the other features of the disease pattern.

It should be noted that the development of anorexia nervosa is related to the interactions between individual characteristics, family environment, and the wider social environment. No single component can be identified as the exclusive cause (Fassino, Amianto, and Abbate-Daga, 2009). However, it seems evident in any case that the cultural setting is significantly influential because this phenomenon seems to be practically unknown in areas where the availability of food is very scarce, a fact that may suggest that the disease has a cultural and social basis as well.

At the individual level, a person is often conflicted between the sense of weakness, inadequacy, low self-esteem, and fasting. The latter helps the individual feel strong and offers the illusion of self-control. Some social factors can certainly facilitate the development of the sense of inadequacy underlying this pathology. For instance, the beauty standards and physical attractiveness of models as presented by mass media are often characteristic of a small segment of the population. In addition, technology and special effects are employed to make the images approximate the ideal. Such perfected imageries significantly facilitate self-comparisons and result in increasing changes in the personal image expectations of individuals (Blowers et al., 2003). Thus, the images propagated in the mass media can become problematic for women, particularly for preadolescent and adolescent female individuals. The sight of beautiful and thin super-models in advertisements can create self-doubt and dissatisfaction in many female individuals concerning their faces and bodies. This dynamic can undermine their self-confidence, and they may consequently indulge in unhealthy eating practices associated with eating disorders (Freedman, 1984).

In fact, anorexia nervosa often begins with the idea that being thinner is equivalent to being more beautiful (an idea encouraged by Western cultures). The individual is constantly cognizant of this notion and is pushed to the extreme, leading to the absence of reality checks and the development of an obsession. An altered perception of the body image is thus developed.

As previously noted, the feeling of inadequacy is counterbalanced by fasting because anorexic individuals imagine not eating represents a solution to their personal problems. The anorexic patient experiences a strong sense of guilt if dieting is interrupted, and this is often accompanied by a strong sense of existential emptiness and loneliness. Frequently, there also exists a lack of emotional self-regulation. Further, the risk of tendencies toward eating disorders is associated with low self-esteem, body dissatisfaction, and discontent with one's overall appearance (Kim and Lennon, 2007).

9 Nervous Bulimia and Binge Eating Disorder
A Contemporary Overview

9.1 NERVOUS BULIMIA

The internalization of a lean body ideal has been found to increase the risk of developing bulimia nervosa, a disorder characterized by a disturbed body image, repetitive binge eating, and compensatory behaviors, such as self-induced vomiting, laxative abuse, or fasting (Anitha et al., 2019). Binge eating or bulimic crises are characterized by the ingestion of an exaggerated amount of food in a short time (less than two hours) in comparison with what most people would eat in such duration under similar circumstances (Anitha et al., 2019; Sanavio and Cornoldi, 2001; APA, 2013).

The person loses control during the binge eating episode, cannot stop eating, and cannot regulate what and how much is eaten. The episode ends because there is nothing left to eat or because the individual feels overstuffed and sick. This phenomenon is very different from an instance of gluttony; it is typified by the ingestion of excessive quantities of food rather than a focus on the quality of the ingested food. In most cases, bulimic crises occur in solitude and in secret precisely because those suffering from this disorder are usually ashamed of it and endeavor to keep those who live with them unaware of their condition (Anitha et al., 2019; Sanavio and Cornoldi, 2001; APA, 2013).

Overeating can be induced by depressive moods, conditions of interpersonal stress, and feelings of dissatisfaction. Overeating is often the consequence of hunger accumulated through fasting and the rigid restrictions the individual self-imposes on their food ingestion. An episode of overindulging could cause a binge-eater a momentary decrease of the depressed disposition, but the person usually subsequently displays shame, cruel self-criticism, and a resurgence of despondency (Anitha et al., 2019; Sanavio and Cornoldi, 2001; APA, 2013).

Such episodes can also be observed in some instances of anorexia nervosa but are more typical of bulimia nervosa, a distinct eating disorder. Notably, anorexia nervosa is more common in adolescents, whereas bulimia nervosa and binge eating disorder are less prevalent in the pediatric age (Suciu and Crișan, 2020). An increasing number of cases are now diagnosed with bulimia nervosa or binge eating disorder (Hay et al., 2017; Udo and Grilo, 2018).

The essential manifestations of bulimia nervosa are binge eating accompanied by certain compensatory measures to prevent the consequent weight gain, including self-induced vomiting after an episode of overeating, which is a commonly adopted technique. Vomiting reduces the physical discomfort of being overfed and decreases the fear of gaining weight. Other compensatory measures that may be taken for overeating are fasting over the following days, physical exercise, excessive use of laxatives, and other activities that interfere with a person's normal life routine. Just like people who develop anorexia nervosa, individuals who develop bulimia nervosa accord disproportionate importance to weight and body shape. These factors affect their levels of self-esteem in a direct and excessive manner (APA, 2013). On a general level, Kim and Lennon (2007) state, "Studies show that most women are likely to perceive themselves as overweight regardless of their actual weight and are more likely to be dissatisfied with their bodies because of distorted perceptions of body size" (p. 7).

As with anorexia nervosa, the proportion of female individuals to male individuals is around 10:1 with respect to the prevalence of this disorder (APA, 2013). This condition can lead to serious consequences, as Anitha et al. (2019) also emphasize, saying, "Bulimia nervosa was ranked 12th leading cause of disability adjusted life years ... in females aged 15–19 years in high-income group countries out of 306 mental and physical disorders" (p. 1).

To summarize, the specific diagnostic criteria proposed by *DSM-V* (APA, 2013) to identify bulimia nervosa are as follows:

A. Recurrent episodes of overeating: An overeating episode is characterized by both the duration and the quantity of food ingested. Those suffering from bulimia nervosa feel they have no control and eat significantly larger amounts of food than the majority of individuals would consume in the same time and under similar circumstances.

B. Recurrent and inappropriate compensatory behaviors to prevent weight gain: Bulimia nervosa patients may self-induce vomiting, fast, undertake excessive physical exercise, or abuse laxatives, diuretics, or other medications.

C. Regularity of episodes: Overeating and inappropriate compensatory behaviors occur on average at least once a week for three months.

D. Self-esteem levels are unduly influenced by body shape and weight.

E. The alteration does not occur exclusively during episodes of anorexia nervosa.

DSM-V further states that the prevalence of this disorder is higher among young adults. It is also necessary to specify that bulimia nervosa usually begins in adolescence or early adulthood. Its onset before puberty or after the age of forty is rare. Overeating usually begins during or after a period of dietary restrictions, and in many stressful situations, overeating can be related to the onset of this disease. It has also been found that individuals who experience a phase of anorexia nervosa during the course of the disease usually return to a state of bulimia nervosa and are likely to alternate between these two disorders multiple times (APA, 2013).

Bulimia nervosa occurs with approximately similar prevalence in most industrialized countries such as the United States, Canada, Europe, Australia, Japan, New Zealand, and South Africa (APA, 2013). However, Anitha et al. (2019) also specify that "eating disorders appear to be increasing in Asian and Arab countries in conjunction with increasing industrialization, urbanization and globalization" (p. 2).

This fact seems to confirm the importance of cultural and social influences on the development of this problem (Anitha et al., 2019).

9.2   BINGE EATING

We must also note that a subgroup of individuals with bulimia nervosa continue to overeat but no longer execute inappropriate compensatory conduct (i.e., vomiting). Thus, their symptoms often satisfy the
criteria for another disorder, binge eating. Diagnosis should, in any
event, be based on the current clinical manifestation, for instance,
considering the past three months (APA, 2013).

DSM-V sets the following diagnostic criteria for the binge eating
disorder:

A. Recurrent binge eating episodes: A binge eating episode is characterized by
    eating significantly more food than most people would eat in the same
    timeframe, coupled with the sense of loss of control during the episode.
B. Binge eating episodes are associated with three or more of the following
    aspects: eating much faster than normal; eating until one feels
    unpleasantly full; eating large quantities of food even when one does not
    feel hungry; eating alone because of the embarrassment of how much one
    is eating; feeling disgusted with oneself; and feeling depressed or very
    guilty about the episode.
C. There is marked discomfort with regard to binge eating.
D. Binge eating occurs, on average, at least once a week for three months.
E. Binge eating is not associated with the systematic implementation of
    inappropriate compensatory behavior, as in bulimia nervosa, and does not
    occur exclusively during bulimia nervosa or anorexia nervosa.

Recurrent overeating is thus a common phenomenon between binge
eating disorder and bulimia nervosa. However, the former differs from
the latter in some fundamental aspects – in terms of clinical manifestation, the recurrent inappropriate compensatory behaviors observed
in bulimia nervosa (for example, vomiting) are absent.

Unlike individuals affected by bulimia nervosa, people affected
by binge eating disorder do not typically exhibit marked or sustained
dietary restrictions aimed at influencing the weight and body shape
between one binge episode and the other. However, frequent
attempts to follow a diet may be reported (APA, 2013).

Binge eating disorder is also distinguished from bulimia nervosa in terms of responsiveness to treatment: statistically, the improvement rates are much higher for individuals with binge eating disorder than they are for individuals with bulimia nervosa (APA, 2013). However, some common dynamics are observed at the root of both bulimia and binge eating. Kim and Lennon (2007) note, "Among young women, various eating-related problems such as the use of laxatives or diuretics, strict eating restraints, and binge eating are associated with body dissatisfaction" (p. 6).

Notably, binge eating disorder is associated with being overweight and obese but presents several significant characteristics that differ from obesity. First, the levels of overestimation of weight and body shape are greater in obese individuals who indulge in binge eating than it is in those who do not. Second, psychiatric comorbidity rates are significantly higher among obese individuals who binge eat when compared with those who do not. Third, scientific research results reveal a long-term positive outcome of evidence-based psychological treatments for binge eating disorder as opposed to the current absence of effective long-term treatments for obesity (Kim and Lennon, 2007).

Finally, it must be highlighted that each individual case has to be specifically analyzed, and as already stated, it is not possible to attribute the cause of all eating disorders to one single factor. The reasons for the development of such symptoms are vested in the complex interactions between individual, relational, and family-based factors as well as cultural and social features that could involve some risks (Fassino, Amianto, and Abbate-Daga, 2009). For instance, pro-anorexia and pro-bulimia blogs and sites exist paradoxically on the Internet and can dangerously instigate the onset and maintenance of the eating disorder. Such platforms declare, for example, that not being slim means not being attractive, that being slim is much more important than being healthy, etc. (It should be emphasized that such sites are now illegal in some countries.)

10 Contemporary Perspectives on Obesity

10.1 OBESITY: A CONTEMPORARY OVERVIEW

Big Girl you are beautiful!

(Mika [Michael Holbrook Penniman, Jr.], "Big Girl," 2008)

Several psychological factors may play a role in the etiology and course of many cases of obesity (Molinari and Castelnuovo, 2012). It has been noted above that this clinical condition does not appear within the classification of mental disorders because extant research has not ascertained the constant association of obesity with any psychological or behavioral syndrome (APA, 2013).

Obesity involves a complex interweaving of factors. The side effects of some psychotropic drugs significantly contribute to the development of obesity, which represents a risk factor for the development of some mental disorders such as depression (APA, 2013). It must also be remembered that the association between obesity and binge eating seems strongly correlated to the development of psychopathology (Molinari and Castelnuovo, 2012). It is, therefore, a matter worthy of intensive examination:

How is obesity related to a person's identity?
How does the situation vary with gender?
How does the condition vary with age?

A general overview suggests that low self-esteem, body image disorders, and poor social contact frequently occur in obese people (Molinari and Castelnuovo, 2012). Scientific research has confirmed the common notion that obese people are often subjected to stigma, prejudice, and discriminatory behaviors precisely for their appearance and that this stance is particularly accentuated in Westernized countries (Puhl and Brownell, 2001). It is, hence, logical to assume that part of the psychological discomfort that obese individuals suffer is related to the negative effects of such discrimination based on identity (Molinari and Castelnuovo, 2012).

The prejudice toward overweight people persists, and it is very marked today despite the growing numbers of obese people and the discovery that some genetic contributions may be related to this condition. However, discrimination against people who are overweight prevails in all age groups, reconfirming the encouragement of Western societies to attain the ideal of thinness and its stigmatization of those who deviate from its canons. The data in this regard are shocking. A group of six-year-old children labeled an overweight child shown in images as "lazy," "dirty," "stupid," "ugly," "cheater," and "one who tells lies." The stigma associated with obesity can continue through adolescence and remain unchanged even following the individual's entry into adulthood. For example, a group of university students stated that obese individuals were less desirable as marital partners than were scammers, cocaine addicts, and pickpockets (Molinari and Castelnuovo, 2012).

Such negative social attitudes toward obese people seem pervasive. The unfair treatment reserved for overweight people, particularly women, has actually been noted in all employment aspects – personnel selection, placement, remuneration, promotion, and dismissal (Roheling, 1999). The factors involved in this context vary; for example, from a family perspective, communication is often lacking in contexts where there is an obese child, and some difficulties are observed in the expression of emotions, particularly negative feelings (Molinari and Castelnuovo, 2012). This finding throws up another factor that can create certain difficulties for overweight individuals and relates to both the causes and the effects of the condition of obesity.

10.2   OBESITY AND IDENTITY

The importance people accord to the reactions of other individuals can cause them to define themselves in relation to others, exerting an impact on their personal identity. Thus, prejudice and discrimination can become chronic stressors that influence every aspect of a person's life and affect the development of personal identity. An obese person often creates a specific identity unrelated to the individual's actual qualities and characteristics (Clerici, Gabrielli, and Vanotti, 2010).

Obese individuals also reveal higher levels of personality characteristics linked to the "novelty search" scale than people with normal weight do, and they attain low self-directivity scores (Molinari and Castelnuovo, 2012). They may be unable to control their impulses to eat and are very attracted to food stimuli in their continuous search for constant and renewed gratification through food, which supposedly distracts them from other matters.

One could then consider what changes may occur in the identity of an obese individual if that person is able to lose extra weight. Oftentimes, difficulties may arise or an actual crisis requiring the person to deal with new demands from the environment such as increasing attention from the opposite sex. A partner may become quite jealous and try to interfere with the weight loss process. Paradoxically, the social environment surrounding the individual (which earlier discriminated against the person for the extra weight) is then not always ready or receptive to this change despite the fact that the social environment itself had previously communicated to the individual the unacceptability of that person's previous bodily state (Clerici et al., 2010). Once again, some contradictory messages are exchanged.

The change in body morphology can also correspond to a modification in the person's attitude, and the individual may get many more opportunities for sexual encounters. Adaptation to the new condition is often abrupt, and slimming down may represent the simultaneous reappropriation and loss of one's identity (Molinari and Castelnuovo, 2012).

Formerly obese people may relate unreasonably to others after slimming and become aggressive or unable to optimally regulate their emotional reactions, probably because they become partially disoriented (Molinari and Castelnuovo, 2012). Obesity also appears to encompass a defensive valence. Consistent weight loss may constitute the removal of the overweight armor; hence, the individual must learn anew to relate to others as an equal in his or her new condition because the obesity-related impediments and handicaps are no longer present. The physical and psychological environmental demands then become identical to those expected of any normal-weighing individual. Frequently, a person may not feel able to meet all these new demands after losing weight, never having had the opportunity to get used to them (Molinari and Castelnuovo, 2012).

In addition, a person may face the effects of food disinhibition if the individual remains unable to sense self-appreciation after all the sacrifices that have been made to lose the extra weight. This inability often results in the quick recovery of the lost weight, activating the perverse yo-yo effect (Garner, 1991). The rapid weight gain that often occurs after a diet may be even greater than at the starting point.

Weight loss is therefore not just a physical issue; it has much more profound implications. It determines radical changes in the cognitive attitude toward food with respect to one's body and the surrounding environment (Molinari and Castelnuovo, 2012). Such changes can be harmonious and well-integrated into the subject identity, or they can be exhausting enough to activate an identity crisis. Indeed, significant identity changes may occur. Conspicuous weight loss can cause immense transformations in a person's somatic morphology, which can trigger difficulties in elaborating and adapting because the body pattern and body image may be distorted.[1]

---

[1] Sometimes, difficulties related to the discrepancy between expectations and realistic results also arise. For further details, see Molinari and Castelnuovo (2012).

Weight loss can further manifest preexisting psychological problems and make some interpersonal ties less balanced. Some relationships may be consolidated; others may break down. For instance, conflict may be observed in the life of a couple because the person who has lost weight may become more autonomous and assertive; perhaps, the presence of an inhibited member was a prerequisite for the continuation of the relationship.

In addition, the body patterns established in the past on the basis of the somatic morphology of an obese person no longer find correspondence in the data emanating from the body after weight loss. Often, previously overweight individuals continue to move clumsily as though they were obese. They are unable to govern their movements, and some of them feel physically insecure (Molinari and Castelnuovo, 2012). Much ambivalence is, therefore, unleashed.

10.3   OBESITY AND GENDER

What happens with obesity in different age groups and genders?

The obesity phenomenon can reveal completely peculiar dynamics in the child phase. The overweight boy generally harbors a positive image of himself. He sees himself as robust and strong, and therefore he feels capable of overwhelming others. This aspect of the gender stereotype is what a male usually desires, but the situation changes radically when the child becomes obese. He tends to see himself as unattractive because he encounters difficulties and awkwardness in his movement and faces considerable marginalization. For example, he can no longer play football/soccer, and sometimes his classmates make fun of him. This transitioning from one condition to the other often occurs in just a few months. Sometimes, all the child requires is a restorative visit to a grandparent for a couple of weeks (see Clerici et al., 2010).

Conversely, the overweight female child immediately begins to show difficulties with her body. This effect can also be correlated to gender stereotypes. She reacts adversely to the appearance of cellulite or the fat distribution that distinguishes her from other girls even when the physical change is extremely limited (Clerici et al., 2010).

The expression of such concerns by little girls must be heeded even at this stage because these feelings represent a real and serious problem for them even if they are not yet at the pathological stage. Unfortunately, both parents and family doctors often place little importance on this discomfort and do not offer the girls any advice that might be helpful. Thus, they lose the opportunity to make a timely intervention that might eliminate both the unease and the risks to the physical and mental health of the girls. A clarification must be made here. A particularly interesting result of research concerning obese female children reveals that they do not have a negative self-image (which is instead more frequent in obese adult women); in fact, they commonly find respite in a new situation where they feel particularly protected. They progressively enclose themselves within just a few environments: at home with family, at grandparents', or with a few friends, always the same, where the girls feel accepted and reassured (Clerici et al., 2010).

One should not at this point think that the girls have simply surrendered; on the contrary, most of the girls do not want to lose weight and feel as though they have reached an ideal situation that allows them to live more securely without the need to measure up to the stimuli and potential frustrations that are imposed from the outside world. These are girls who stay at home most of the time and do not want to go out because they like staying with their families. In this sense, the family environment is paradoxically likely to become entrapping and symbiotic as often happens also for people who develop anorexia (Clerici et al., 2010).

While it is a terrible thing to state, it seems some families unconsciously need one of their members to be kept under control at all times; unfortunately, a weak child can also present an excellent opportunity for parents to feel indispensable and avoid the sense of abandonment that can arise when the child becomes more autonomous. In a similar vein, one could ask whether an obese partner in the adult couple can make the other spouse feel more confident of never being abandoned. Parents can suffer from a strong sense of uselessness upon the emancipation of their children. If a partner can prevent the weight loss of an adult, for minors, it can be their relatives. All such dynamics can take place at an unconscious level; for example, a fifteen-year-old obese girl who remains extremely overweight will never rebel against her parents because she wants to go on vacation to the beach with her friends. She will give her parents the great satisfaction of going to the mountains with them.

Even if the parents become convinced at a conscious level that they want their daughter to become independent and openly declare that they want her growth and autonomy, they maintain these often symbiotic dynamics at the unconscious level. In actuality, many families encompass complex and established balances that no one wants to undermine. For example, in some instances, a sibling of an obese child who is beginning to lose weight may clearly display a concern that the weight loss could lead to unpleasant changes. Perhaps such siblings are primarily afraid of losing their freedom if their parents stopped worrying almost exclusively about the obese girl who has hitherto absorbed almost all their energy (Clerici et al., 2010).

Once again, a paradox becomes apparent. Adolescents are increasingly tormented by the obsession with the perfect body, and at the same time, childhood obesity is a relevant and very present phenomenon that is linked to great risks. People tend to retain this condition largely unconsciously. This opposition does not seem strange per se because, as we have seen above, ambivalence and paradoxes that often become contradictions are the prerogatives of the hypermodern era.[2]

Finally, Clerici et al. (2010) offer some remarks that are worth considering here:

> For the Pythagoreans, medicine is really "medietas," according to the etymological reconstruction of Isidore of Seville in his

---

[2]   In this sense, F. Riva (2015) speaks of "obese city" and "slender city."

Etymologiae or *Origines,* or "right measure," a balance between the parts, psychophysical "rightness" in the sign of totality.

The dominant culture today is poles apart from that of the Pythagoreans in respect of the most common daily behaviors, and that applies to the field of nutrition too.

To prevent the genuine suffering caused by two opposing forms of excess, i.e. obesity and anorexia, continuing to increase in new generations, it is essential to recalibrate the Greek exhortation to the "right measure" in respect of young peoples' experiences.

We must go back to Plato's *Republic,* which is truly enlightening: "and do you not think it indecent – he writes – having to resort to medicine not because of wounds or seasonal diseases, but for our sloth or for malnutrition?" [...] Aristoxenus, for his part, also underlines the following: "Since childhood, one must behave in an orderly way also when it comes to food, teaching that order and measure are beautiful and beneficial, disorder and excess are repulsive and harmful."

(Clerici et al., 2010, p. 150)

This excerpt refers to the Pythagorean era and demonstrates how the value of the balanced measure (of the "right middle ground") was highlighted, a phenomenon that appears extremely anachronistic juxtaposed with the hypermodern obsession with thinness and with certain typical and controversial attitudes toward food in our times.

Evidently, the ideals of desirability change from era to era; this perspective can be applied both to the relationship with food and to the ideal of beauty. For example, numerous ancient Egyptian illustrations representing women in a maternal role showcase the ideal of the female form in that time. The beauty ideal in classical Greece was exemplified by the harmonious agreement between a body's parts vis-à-vis the body as a whole: a body was deemed attractive when all its parts were proportioned to its length. In ancient Rome, opulent women were considered beautiful; hence, beauty was typified by rich and luxurious clothes and a lot of jewelry and makeup, which also represented the magnificence of Roman imperial life. Until a few decades ago, a beautiful woman was curvaceous, as also observed in previous centuries. A look at Impressionist paintings elucidates that Renoir's female beauty was full-bodied. Clerici et al. (2010) summarize, "In most of the past centuries what has happened today has not happened; as a matter of fact, in our days we can speak of a real dictatorship of only one imperative: to be thin" (p. 96).

In global terms, it is certain that cultures evolve and transform over time in all their aspects (Garano, Dettori, and Barucca, 2016). It is evident that many things have now changed from how they were in previous periods, such as the human perspective on aesthetics, food, and the body, all of which are presently structured in ways radically different from those in the past, in particular in Western societies.

Now particularly apparent at various levels is the influence of opposed and contradictory forces. Anorexia is spreading in tandem with obesity. The human relationship with food is progressively characterized on the basis of incongruous and clashing trends. For example, fast and slow foods stand side by side on supermarket aisles. Behaviors range from the systematic refusal of food to the obsessive seeking and selection of foods to favor and avoid (Garano et al., 2016). The contemporary dynamics oscillate between the quest for extreme experiences and the need for stability and safety, and between the exhibition of valued corporeality, divinized and displayed at all costs, and the simultaneous proposition of subjecting the body to progressive torture. When one loses weight, one submits to cosmetic surgery to improve oneself; when one has had cosmetic surgery performed, one uses photo editing to showcase oneself better (because one is never perfect). In terms of the broader social context, we can once again note some opposing drives that could be highlighted by the conflict inherent in the need expressed by youngsters for autonomous spaces away from their family and origins and the existential and work precariousness that often forces children to stay connected to parents (Clerici et al., 2010). Many contradictions are now evident.

All this happens in the context of a truly complex and paradoxical reality, wherein the family often plays an increasingly entangling role by maintaining some dangerous pathological balances. As noted above, this process becomes evident in problematic situations where people consciously or unconsciously contribute to the maintenance of risky physical conditions, like obesity, in themselves or their children; this seems to be the other face of the contemporary obsession with achieving the perfect body. It is further confirmation of the present-day centrality of the body. In fact, a perverse and disturbing identification has now been generated between self-care and body care – the need to correct one's shape and one's physical aspect irrespective of the cost to one's health. Similarly, in this regard, the culture of consumerism induces us to forget our sense of limits, specifically the right measure, in our diets as well.

Humans change in ways that reflect the times in which they exist, and times change according to human societies and their dynamics. In 1400, Pico della Mirandola aptly wrote of the human being as resembling a chameleon. Unlike all other beings, human nature is indeterminate, and individuals can thus shape their lives on the basis of autonomous choices. They can decide what to become, angels or beasts, without prejudice to the gap between aspiration and reality (Clerici et al., 2010).

PART IV Which Possible Horizons? Some Final Considerations

11 Body Image, Narcissisms, and Depression

11.1 AFFECTS AND HEALTHY DETACHMENT

> From the "sociobiological" point of view, according to an opinion, the human being is, by nature, called "a social animal" in that they must deal with other people, feel part of a group, and maintain relationships.
>
> (Frati, 2012, p. 165)

According to Massimo Recalcati and Jean-Luc Nancy, the human being may not be naturally inclined to self-sacrifice. Our existence can be lived and shared with other people but can never be tortured or sacrificed (Nancy, 2002; Recalcati, 2017). In other words, we are naturally disposed toward self-preservation efforts because our existential energy is unique and cannot be reduced by any force except to safeguard ourselves and others.

> On the other hand, even psychoanalytic theory itself, from Freud onwards, has always focused on the importance of the so-called "life drives," i.e. those forces that push individuals to preserve themselves as a living organism and to relate to others for the research of mutual aggregation.
>
> (Frati, 2012, p. 166)

Then again, according to Levinás (1990, p. 135), we are now asked to perform a continuous paradoxical sacrifice and seek perpetual and self-centered enjoyment imposed by the law of consumerism, the doctrine of which is "You have to achieve pleasure!" Increasingly, this dictum encroaches upon personal security, injects melancholic moods,[1] or

---

[1]   For further details, see Recalcati (2019, p. xi). According to this work, we have moved forward, from a capitalism full of compulsive consumerism and aimed at pervasive enjoyment, toward conservative forms of existence aimed at individual security. The

contrarily triggers an (often-fake) exhibition of happiness.[2] The law of consumerism often also invites nonstop efficiency and mandates the apparent (hypocritical) removal of any conflict.

Human beings frequently fail to attend to other human beings (and their mysteries, secrets, and modesties) in societies replete with perfect shapes (of bodies and things in general). In such cultures, everything appears to be linear, shiny, and immaculate (like the screens of some smartphones), and the lack of conflict and absence of the disturbing aspects of life (such as aging and death, as previously noted) is generally apparent. According to Han (2018), the digital dimension also eliminates all forms of interplay between physical closeness and emotional nearness. Nowadays, technology and new forms of communication enable everything to exist at the same time and equally close or distant. Digital society often deprives the world of mystery. Hyper-nearness and hyper-exposure (for example, through mass media images that do not show any modesty or decency) frequently destroy appropriate and healthy distances between people. All bodies look identical in such vulgar representations.

The recovery of a balanced distance imposes itself with absolute urgency as the optimal way of relating to others. According to Frati (2012), "The path of structuring emotional relationships goes from birth to maturity and has as an ideal goal the conquest of the ability to establish a balanced, lasting and mutually appreciated relationship with another person" (p. 169).

The individual of our times is usually narcissistic and depressed, apparently full of (fake) positivity, and often unable to see the negative aspects of life (which are photoshopped just as a picture might be).

---

2   prevailing attitude of the individual is no longer one of a frantic rush toward objects of enjoyment but one of self-conserving closure typical of a neo-melancholic folding.
On "the obligation to be happy" as the dominant ideology of our times, see Bruckner (2001).

This person constantly thinks to measure and calculate everything, which is detrimental to human desire (and its creative tension when desire is sublimated). The contemporary dictatorship of exhibitionism, wherein everything is exposed, enjoyed, and controlled, has contributed to our losing sight of the uniqueness of other human beings and the mysteries of social interactions (i.e., everything is now displayed on social media).

> Conversely, according to Buber (1993), the principle of being an individual is based on consciousness of the original and natural distance from other human beings. One positions oneself as another person, not as an object, transcending one's ego, which, seizing the distance, hesitates, questions itself, and opens itself to the tension required to refrain from objectifying other people. In fact, love is a movement aroused in the soul by a person, who therefore ends up being involved in feeling somehow related to them (Frati, 2012). However, according to Han (2015c), there is, metaphorically, "too much proximity" where another person is concerned. Under such circumstances, a person then becomes akin to an object for pure enjoyment and is treated as a tool for a need to be satisfied; worse, the person is regarded as an exposed object to be sexualized. Such metaphoric proximity is negative. Nevertheless, the dissolution of a healthy distance among persons is common now; however, such a negation of distance does not lead to deeper intimacy among human beings. On the contrary, any closeness is eliminated. As Frati (2012, pp. 175–176) notes: "Think, for example, of the disconcerting phenomenon of stalking or domestic violence, which in our country in general, and in those countries belonging to the so-called industrialized West, but certainly also well beyond it, is a social emergency." Instead of healthy constructive proximity, a harmful absence of distance now exists in respect of other people (Han, 2017b).
>
> We will now make a brief reference to healthy detachment, as an important piece of advice for human beings today and as a message

to be communicated to our children. Well, healthy detachment is opposed to selfishness, possession, and egoism. It should not be confused with the most terrible of feelings, indifference, but it must be seen and calibrated in everyday life … in other words, healthy detachment is a balanced sharing, a passionate involvement in reality, precisely because it is not the egoistic possession that counts … In this way, we will no longer be slaves of things, and of the conflicting feelings that their possession arouse, but instead, we will be free, open to all that truly humanizes us.

(Clerici, Gabrielli, and Vanotti, 2010, p. 87)

Thus, when balanced and healthy distance/detachment is abolished, there can be no respect in the relationship and this may result in an unhealthy, symbiotic relationship with individuality and different needs unexpressed.

Biopower practices (which we talked about in the Chapter 1) now include certain social surveillance techniques that describe how our bodies should be governed, how we should have sex, feed ourselves correctly, live healthy and sporty lives, and exist in a regulated way. The dynamics of counter-power also inhabit the social system and trigger certain processes. With the contemporary approach to the body where no healthy distance exists between people, it is difficult to harmonize sexual performance and tenderness because people are often treated like objects or simply as soulless bodies (the pornography point of view). As Frati (2012, p. 182) notes:

Today the experience of falling in love seems to tend to assume the typical connotations of a sort of mercantile exchange with respect to particularly desirable and desired personal and social characteristics, in which more or less unconsciously everyone tries to obtain the best and most convenient things that reality can offer.

By contrast Frati (2012) asserts that "the ability to really love is like a virtuous exchange rather than a need to be satisfied or a fear of loneliness" (p. 184).

Only if in caressing and touching another person's body there is a place for real intimacy, decency, mystery, and secrecy (Irigaray, 2013) is one able to relate to the other person with the appropriate distance and modesty,[3] enabling healthy Eros as a desire never objectified. Thus, one does not use other people as tools for the fulfillment of selfish needs; rather, one respects others. Frati (2012) thus states, "True and mature love is based on extremely advanced processes, as they are based on a relational mode of constructive exchange and mutual enrichment" (p. 189).

There is no opposition, no exercise of dominion, no mere projection of oneself in a healthy relationship with another person. This association is not a calculation; it is, rather, the metaphorical sacred place where one can entrust one's weaknesses to regain one's elevation. This dynamic can be correlated to the following:

> the idea for which love is above all focused on is giving and not receiving. However, in this sense giving does not mean giving something in the logic of sacrificing oneself, or a part thereof, nor even giving to receive something in return, but it is an enrichment that brings a sense of vitality and joy. In this condition, individuals maintain their freedom; they are the masters of their affection: giving of oneself therefore does not mean an impoverishment, a loss of oneself, but, on the contrary, expresses maximum valorization.
>
> (Frati, 2012, p. 191)

It is ultimately a sort of mystic migration process in the ability of the ego to migrate from itself that detachment is measured as a radical awareness of the finiteness of every determination, starting from one's own will. It represents a sort of dematerialization of the ego into a more spiritual dimension to attain a new point of view on the Absolute.

Appropriately recontextualized, the mystical theoretical concept mooted in particular by Meister Eckhart and Angelo Silesio opens our mindsets to the metaphorical death of the soul, or of the

---

[3] E. Levinás in this sense speaks of the relationship with the other as a "game with something slipping away" (1989, p. 55).

"small self," which is all frenzy, productivity, and consumption. This demise seems to connote the contemporary man in an increasingly widespread manner, a situation wherein the ego grasps things to appropriate them and to seal them in itself by exchanging restlessness as research with restlessness as manipulative frenzy (Vannini, 2003).

In this sense, an anthropological reorientation of the human relationship with time is needed to replace "suspended time." Bauman (2008) opined that technological societies cognize pointillist (atomized) time, which is incohesive and divided into disconnected eternal instants; it is bound to the ideology of the present, immediate fruition, enjoyment of performance, and excess.

On the other hand, suspended time is a time of restlessness. As Han (2012) asserts, "It is you who makes time! The clock's spheres are senses: stop the time scale and time is gone" (p. 47). The play on words is paradigmatic and is thus recontextualizable. Suspend your time, abandon your doing, and abandon the time for your will for power, and make yourself restless to the other, that Absolute, who, in the erotic act, fills you while emptying you, enriches you while impoverishing you, and paradoxically metaphorically announces your death while offering you life.

Eros thus implies the ability to see in the other person the irreducibility of one's identity and completeness. It is not viewed, as in the positivizing and equalizing technological society, as the mere expressive flesh of a continuous flow that is volatile and never witnessed by a conclusive decision that can ultimately claim, "Your identity is Absolute, concluded, it can never be something undecided." The words of Han superbly confirm this pattern:

> the subject dies in the Other but a return to oneself follows this
> death. However, the return reconciled with oneself from the Other
> is by no means a violent appropriation of the Other ... Rather, it is
> the gift of the Other, which presupposes abandonment, the
> renunciation of oneself.
>
> *(Han, 2012, p. 47)*

Resetting one's life to self-renunciation signifies abandoning the healthy realism of our times, which basically coincides with emotional indifference, if not cynicism (Zamperini, 2007). In other words, one must now be plastic.

In fact, the praise of plasticity represents another interesting standpoint. Contemporary humanity seems inhabited by flexibility more than plasticity. The term "flexibility" indicates the dynamics of docility with which a person adapts to existential rules now imposed by society. It is a process that frequently lacks creativity and is devoid of the courage to say "no." It denotes a mood without any philosophical asceticism (De Monticelli, 1995; Tagliapietra, 2009), supported by the intimidating nature of contemporary reality. This dynamic therefore deprives the real human self of certain possibilities such as those of surprise, the unexpected, and the creative advent of many perspectives.

We are also now becoming interchangeable, removable, and recomposable individuals to an extent.[4] We have modular biographies, wherein modules are replaced with continuously fluidizable useful units. This fact is particularly applicable to young people who are subjected to the constant evaluation (Del Rey, 2018) of their performances, who become "perfect machines," and whose performances are always visible, calculable, and optimal:

> In reality, this new injunction to fluidity and flexibility, so praised
> by small and medium-sized industrialists, as by politicians and
> governments, has very dangerous implications ... The elderly
> person is too metaphorically "sculpted" to dissolve in this fluidity,
> which makes it necessary to learn and unlearn incessantly. The

[4]   Foucault (1998, p. 183) prefers to use the term "subjectivation" rather than "subject" to
indicate the historical process that administers, manages, governs, controls, and directs
the subject and its relevant device, i.e., the technical process, from word to its concrete
structure and from said to unspoken. The subject itself is created through this process.
Simondon (2011), on the other hand, prefers to use the term "identification" to express
a material, specific historical form of identification. Agamben (2006b) uses both terms
to highlight how the abundance of devices of our time, including "technological
prostheses," leads to a multiplicity of the configurations of the subject.

older you are, the less you can edit your modules, your roots, your structure. On the contrary, a young person is – so they say – "fluidizable" to the extreme: it is possible to take possession of him and shape him.

(Benasayag, 2019, p. 57)

Control over our lives has taken on different contours today when compared with the closed spaces of Foucauldian discipline and surveillance. It has the character aptly described by Gill Deleuze as fluidity, instantaneousness, the continuous mixing of elements to confuse and control the subject in an even more pervasive way. In disciplinary societies, all we had to do was start again; in controlling and controlled societies, we never end up with anything.[5]

Plasticity, on the other hand, refers to nature's dynamics – liveliness, unpredictability, and creative articulations. The Hegelian concept of *Wirklicheit*, the actuality or the totality of reality, references plasticity, a concept clearly present in the preface of the *Phenomenology of the Spirit*.[6] Malabou states that a closer look or a finer ear could effortlessly discover the pressing presence of plasticity in an increasing number of speeches. Far from having said everything, plasticity persistently asks to speak; it appears as an operating scheme with increasing importance in philosophy, art (some artists now explicitly claim the status of "plastics"), genetics, neurobiology, ethnology, or psychoanalysis.[7]

[5]   For further details, see Deleuze (2000). As D'Aurizio. (2018, p. 176) has correctly noted: "While internment societies fragmented and segmented the life of the individual, both spatially and chronologically, through their continuous and progressive passage from one institution to another (family-school-barracks-factory-hospital-prison), in control societies the fluidification of space and time draws a situation of 'continuous training' that keeps the subject permanently under pressure."

[6]   For further details, see Malabou (2005). See also Isetta (2015). On the nexus between plasticity and reality, see Agamben (2006a).

[7]   For further details, see Malabou (2000, 2009). We allude to the plasticity of the brain, or of incessant brain remodeling thanks to plastic changes that allow it to continuously review its operational controls by providing it with pockets of environmental and cultural information from which to draw. For further details, see Merzenich (2013) and Siegel (2013).

In Han's refined analysis, creative plasticity is open to the possible, able to live up to the negative, contradiction, and split, in view of continuous remodulations of reality and its possibilities. Openness to creative plasticity occurs when the negative of the otherness is present; consequently, it is eclipsed where the positive, equal, and standardized reign. This aspect is now obliterated in favor of what is positive, unique, and indisputable, that is, the monolithic and intimidating character of what exists.

Paradoxically, according to Han (2015b), depression fully embodies the excess of positivity: Neuronal violence did not originate from negativity extraneous to the system. It is itself rather a systemic violence, that is to say, immanent to the system. Both depression and attention deficit hyperactivity disorder (ADHD) refer to an excess of positivity (and of activity). According to Han (2015b, pp. 9–10), the prefix "hyper" in hyperactivity is not an immunological category but represents only a stereotyping of the positive.

Ultimately, it is difficult to immunize metaphorically in an era where a person is oftentimes evaluated only on the basis of achieved successes and exhibited objects, that is, by products voraciously consumed in an instant, pre-established enjoyment, the aesthetics of the body, and the incorporation of standardized foods. Everything occupies the undifferentiated territory of equals and of the positive without comparison, otherness, or conflict. Overall, it appears difficult to defend or protect ourselves or make our lives unique and unrepeatable events. It is problematic to say no to a reality that imposes homogeneous forms of enjoyment and standardization.

A possible way to implement metaphorical immunological practices and to protect our uniqueness from the uniform codes of our time may be vested in the culture of the body. With particular reference to the younger generations, such an ethos could encourage a possible dialog with ourselves and with the world under the influence of a vital and urgent centrality of feelings and sentimental education.

I I.2   THE IMPORTANCE OF COMMUNICATION
IN A NARCISSISTIC ERA

It is also important to analyze the importance of communication. According to Heidegger, we are not language but conversation. This statement underlines the interactive dimension of humanity, which constitutes a sort of dialectic of listening and talking. This philosophy is consubstantial with our historical being, which has existed since we entered the world; it is connected with our past, present, and future (Heidegger, 1988). For Heidegger, in other words, the human being is not based merely on language in its structural aspect but rather on its interactive dimension of conversation.

In conversation, communication does not refer to the uniformity of what is being said and the lived experience; it alludes, rather, to dialog, openness to the otherness that has always inhabited us, and dispute. It indicates the ability to say no and to dissent. It signifies standing up as creative biographies by being plastic against the presumed unchangeable character of reality, which comes as a package deal with connected rhetoric of healthy realism that is actually nothing more than the tragic mask of docility. It is related to the constraints of everything that is equal and thus controllable.

The human being is in constant dialog with the world: an individual is always in a conversation and in a relationship with the environment, even with mute objects such as trees:

> With all this the tree remains for me an object, an object in space and time, with its own way and its characteristics. However, by will and by grace together, it can also happen that, by observing the tree, I get involved in the relationship with it, and then the tree is no longer an object. The strength of exclusivity grabbed me. For this reason it is not necessary for me to give up any of my ways of observing. There is nothing that I should neglect to see, to observe, and no knowledge that I should forget. Indeed, it is all there together, image and movement, species and specimen, law and number, inseparably united. Everything that belongs to the tree is there together, its shape

and its mechanics, its colors and its chemistry, its speech with the elements and its speech with the stars, all in total unity. The tree is not an impression, it is not a game of my imagination, it is not a state of mind, but it is a living body in front of me and it is connected with me, as I am with it, just in a different way. Do not try to weaken the meaning of the relationship: relationship is reciprocity.

(Besossi Jussi, 1993, p. 63)

In short, everything is a conversation and a relationship, starting from the senses:

Man cannot exempt himself from experiencing the world, from being constantly crossed and modified by it. The world is the emanation of a body that penetrates it. Between the sensation of things and the sensation of oneself, there is a continuous coming and going: before thinking, there are the senses.

(Le Breton, 2007, p. XI)

The relationship at the origin of the conversation is a feeling[8] made of body, skin,[9] and emotions.[10]

---

[8]   At the origin of knowledge, there is feeling and a sentiment of wonder (see Petrosino, 2012). The connections between feeling, passion, and thought were attested by Heidegger during the summer semester of 1924, which was dedicated to the fundamental concepts of Aristotelian philosophy. Heidegger focuses in particular on Aristotle's rhetoric, especially pathos. Heidegger utilizes the pathos as the persuasive and passionate force of the orator to think intensively about the intertwining of existential affectivity and cognitive tension. Unsurprisingly, these reflections flow into the concept of the "emotional situation" (*Befindlichkeit*) of being and time. This emotional condition, along with pure knowledge, constitutes the privileged ways in an indissoluble intertwining of human beings opening to the multiple ways of being. In summary, knowledge is not assured without affectivity, passion, and feeling (because they are correlated). On this topic, see Curi (2013). Severino (1986) is even more clear about this topic insofar as he sees the feeling of wonder, which is the real origin of philosophy, as a mixture of admiration and terror and an anguished amazement at the unpredictability of the world and its incessant evolution.

[9]   Skin and brain, which are formed in the ectoderm, constitute two fundamental parts of living beings; however, it is from the skin that the affective dynamics of a body are created and structured. In fact, the first form of feeling, the ego's first sensation is epidermal; for example, think of the skin contact between an infant and its mother. On this issue, see Anzieu (2017).

[10] One can reference Damasio's studies and the rich debate they have initiated since the mid-nineties on the fundamental role of emotions. For further details, see Damasio (1994) and (2003).

Likewise, the communal enjoyment of food constitutes a dialog of the senses; it is a relationship, a bodily experience, an exposition of our body to others, a common feeling, an act of sharing skin to skin, and a myriad of sensations on the skin. A communal meal represents a strong existential antidote to the isolated dining imposed by the efficiency and frenetic roles of our times or from the dogmas of the purity of the food tribes:

> The meal is a common ritual, the festive climax of the social bond. Cooking is a peaceful joy, a gift of flavor and sociability towards others to whom time and ingeniousness in the preparation of dishes are devoted. As a counterpart, it requires the gustatory pleasure of the guests and their satiety. The sharing of flavors responds to the pleasure of being together, gathering around one's family group, one's friends, one's community, one's guests, colleagues, neighbors, members of the clan, lineage, etc.
>
> *(Le Breton, 2007, p. 408)*

Nancy (2013) observes that all existence, in all its forms and shapes, is bodily exposure. The body, in its nakedness, in the desire that it always stimulates, is the opening, the space wherein existence itself occurs. It has itself as its object: the body is the body. Existence speaks the language of the body, the skin, its nudity, and its naked manifestation. The greatness of thought is in the simplicity of the decision that turns toward the naked manifestation (Nancy, 1998).

However, this fragile, exposed skin, which we intercept in its extreme nakedness, never coincides with the truth; it overlaps, rather, with the mystery of pure immanence, always overflowing into our inquiring gaze (Nancy, 2009). The nakedness of the skin through which existence speaks to us, and which announces the otherness that inhabits us, is never isolated – it indicates relationship and community. Ferrari and Nancy (2003) state that nudity is not a state of being or a quality; it is always a relationship, rather, multiple simultaneous relationships – with others, oneself, the image, and the absence of an image. According to Ferrari and Nancy, we can rebuild a community that sees the body or the skin as the absolute sign of our weakness, as an entity that knows how to give voice to the dignity of the body and to its relational vocation. A community that knows how to draw subversive landscapes, such as respect, tenderness, and caress, can constitute a possible horizon of the aesthetics of existence and beauty.

We now need a kind beauty that displays endurance, responsibility, loyalty, commitment, and caring about otherness:

> Today nothing has consistency and duration. We are faced with radical contingency, so the nostalgia for what binds a commitment and transcends everyday life awakens. Nowadays, we are experiencing a crisis of beauty precisely because beauty has become an object of pleasure, of "likes," pleasant and comfortable. The salvation of beauty means the salvation of what binds and commits us to responsibility.
>
> *(Han, 2012, p. 97)*

This perspective is one wherein the fragility of beauty becomes an occasion for being a community, which makes the city a home wherein to live. In human relationships, affectivity and feelings are useful conditions for thinking together (see Deleuze and Guattari, 2002).

Our cities are places that simultaneously bring people together and tear them apart. No relationship, community, or sense of belonging is created in cities, but they are nevertheless places for co-feeling. The other often remains in the background in the anonymous and disorienting flow of information,[11] goods, production frenzy, and soulless efficiency. Worse, the other as well fades into inconsequence in the indifference of a gaze used to calculate, survive, excel so as to be

---

[11]   G. Simmel (2011, p. 36) has already underlined how the modern metropolitan individual is centered "on the intensification of nervous life, which is produced by the rapid and uninterrupted alternation of external and internal impressions." On the new form that capitalism has assumed in the sign of immateriality (producing, reproducing, archiving, sending information if it is increasingly pervasive and binding), see Quintarelli (2019).

able to give oneself space and emotional openness. Yet, Lazzarini (2011, p. 98) asserts:

> The city is a "womb," capable of hosting and feeding people, generating encounters, intertwining bonds. The city is "home," "the" place, a sort of regulatory idea for every form of associated life, because it is a place from which one must separate in order to start the new, but to which one always tends to return.

It is, hence, necessary to precisely trace the sort of human geography that makes the city a home to be erected, starting from the education of bodies, warm feelings, and most importantly, tenderness, instead of starting from the premise of a place of exchange, business, or production of goods. We should track how the cityscape oscillates between the contradictory forms of collective isolation and dispersion, poverty and opulence, and access to information and digital illiteracy.

It is a debt we have accrued, particularly in favor of our younger generations. Anthropologist Le Breton posited one of the brightest solutions to the discharge of this debt – to restore legitimate citizenship to freedom of thought, desire, and dignity. One must reinstate the fragile but still extraordinary narration of oneself and of one's world and organically enrich school paths with poetry, music, dance, and theater. Le Breton writes:

> Theater is that symbolic place where the fact of testing oneself before the gaze of others allows one to look at oneself from outside, reflect on one's own way of expressing oneself, on the relationship with one's neighbor, with temporality. On stage one can lose one's pride, but can also take back control over an undone identity. A theatrical workshop carried out with seriousness, like that of Kechiche's movie, is an opportunity for young people to try out characters, which is precisely the peculiarity of adolescence and is normally expressed through the use of consumer products or profiles on social networks. Here, however, they are characters with depth, animated by a common

project, in radical break with the suburban dynamics. Young people show novel facets, free from heaviness, leave their dialectical and behavioral routine to discover with amazement that other infinitely calmer, more serene, at-the-center-of -a-sociality-that-no-longer-requires-constant-bragging-and-aggression relationships are possible in the world ... They change perspective, redefine the relationship with others and experience a real rebirth.

(Gabrielli, Grassi, and Le Breton, 2015, pp. 154–155)

In this extract, Gabrielli refers to a drama workshop depicted in Abdellatif Kechiche's film *La schivata* (2002), wherein a French teacher stages a theatrical representation of Marivaux's play *The Game of Love and Chance* (French: *L'Esquive*) with the help of her high school students who are teenagers from the suburbs of Lille. The young people display the aggressive traits typical of their age and speak a stereotyped, scurrilous, fast, and nervous language. However, when they become steeped in Marivaux's language, they listen, speak slowly, and enjoy the words with pleasure (see Gabrielli et al., 2015). Speaking slowly denotes a center of resistance against the tyranny of the present (the atomized time), existential breathlessness, and urgency as a lifestyle; it represents a taste of life.

According to Han (2015c), digital era society operates through screens, the nature of which is often not "cardiological, but pornographic." It has no pathos or feelings but tends to reveal and exhibit everything. Hence, there is no secret, mystery, modesty, or decency, and ultimately, everything is usable and controllable.

The slowness of the utterance of words, on the other hand, does not produce breathlessness. It does not like the instantaneity of the screen's image that appears and immediately disappears, without affective memory, limiting itself to mere information, or worse, limiting itself to morbid curiosity. If anything, it loves contemplation, dwelling, being patient, taking care of the other, and creating community bonds.

The slowness of words denotes their meditative power, which is embodied in the gesture. The gesture becomes body; it appears like a look of tenderness or a caress (Guanzini, 2017); that is to say, the spirit of the contemporary era expresses itself in the practices of touching as opposed to catching, possessing, or excelling.

11.3   HEALTHY RELATIONSHIPS

It is now appropriate to analyze the importance of tenderness.

The prevalence of negative feelings, fear, hostility, economic (and consequently, existential) precariousness, capitulation, productive frenzy, continuous relational anxiety, and wild demands for performance and productivity is now spreading. In such a scenario, body language is marked by extreme efficiency, slenderness, and the ability to always accelerate to remove any encumbrance from production. Thus, young people frequently experience social withdrawal, a sense of progressive subtraction from life's flows, and that the acquisition of the vital path of experience is denied them.

Therefore, it is necessary to restore attention to the body and recover anthropology that offers the means to reinstate fruitful, mature, and deep human relationships by approaching others in an attentive and respectful way that values the mystery of the other.

Metaphorically, touching the other is always a tension, never a possession and never an occupation. "Respect for the other is a fundamental element of mature, perhaps the most essential thing [...] within a mature couple relationship, no type of domination is possible" (Frati, 2012, pp. 192–193). The other is the untouchable par excellence, i.e., it is never our possession. This approach for otherness, Derrida (2007) states, is designed as a movement the privileged voices of which, in our opinion, are tenderness and caress, which are the silent gestures par excellence.

Tenderness is a symbolic place of welcome. It is a world of flesh that becomes a world of flesh, encounter, recognition, and reciprocity. It has nothing to do with the feel-good, sentimentalist aesthetics of our time, which are artificial, temporary, and inhospitable oases that

we believe pacify the productive, cynical, or indifferent bad conscience that accompanies us through most of our existence.
Tenderness does not even obey commercial or marketing codes. It
does not inhabit the hyper-fast and detached body of today's human
being, who simultaneously consumes tenderness and is alien to it and
to warm contact practices because of the fear of exhibiting vulnerabil-
ities, becoming exposed, and hence becoming violable.

The tenderness of which we speak is a natural feeling; it is poetic
in its existence. It lives in the world and gets dirty with the world; it is
combative, creative, and visionary. It imagines and designs new forms
of existence comprising encounters that are anthropological and ecological in their sustainability, rights, and sharing. It takes the perspective of a constant retreat when faced with the mystery of the other and
the other's uniqueness to make room for itself without contradictions:

> It is therefore a matter of imagining new forms and practices of
> individual and collective experiences grounded in an elementary
> way of feeling, in a "combative tenderness" and in a new poetics of
> relationships. We are dealing here with the current onset of a new
> way of meeting the world, one imagined out of processes of
> recognition and proximity, against the background of the drama of
> lifeless, identity-free, country-free, future-free, citizenship-free and
> community-free stories.
>
> (Guanzini, 2017, p. 218)

Tenderness is a gift of the self.[12] In this sense, touching is departing
from the subject's hegemonic claims and from the rocky, muscular,
performance-based self of our times, and simultaneously, it is the way
out of the drifts of isolation that many young people experience: it is
a culture and pedagogy of mystery.

---

[12] "The caress is not a simple floating touch: it is a fashioning. When I caress another
person, I create their flesh by my caress, with my fingers. The caress is that set of
rituals that incarnates the other ... The caress creates the other as flesh both for me
and for themselves [... It] reveals the flesh by divesting the body of its action, splitting
it off from the possibilities that surround it" (Sartre, 1956, p. 430).

By stroking the other and letting ourselves be caressed, we experience the fragility of the skin, the original voices of the body, the vocabulary of emotions that becomes the grammar of feelings, and the overflowing power that Eros gifts. Eros invites us not to take possession of anything, not to calculate anything, and not to possess anything.

The dialectic between tenderness and caress is a subversive gesture in an era that calculates and evaluates everything on the basis of utility. This interaction occurs in the name of everything that is incalculable, that is unprogrammable and unpredictable, and that makes life an extraordinary narration. This concept is excellently exemplified in the poem "Titano amori intorno" by Alda Merini (1997): A useless caress was enough to turn the world upside down. The caress is a gesture with no economic significance; it is not productive nor is it useful, yet it upturns the world. It allows us to see humanity from another perspective on the basis of warm and welcoming expressions and values.

A caress is always an anthropological symbol of meeting, recognition, and hospitality. The face of the other is not a sign; it does not refer to anything else; it is, if anything, the absence of the world of enjoyment, of the useful end in itself, and of self-referential profit. The face, in the fragility of its skin, metaphorically requires tenderness, and philosophically, it demands absolute responsibility. Lévinas (1985) asserts that "The Other is not close to me in space, or close like a relative, but he approaches me essentially insofar as I feel myself – in so far as I am – responsible for him" (p. 96).

Lévinas positions the face at the center of his philosophical speculation but invites us not to do the same with others: those whom we meet, who challenge us, and who ask us for recognition. The face is a type of portrait to be observed in detail, a phenomenon to be deciphered, a place of mystery and unrepeatable singularity. A particularly significant paragraph is reproduced below:

> I do not know if one can speak of a "phenomenology" of the face, since phenomenology describes what appears. So, too, I wonder if

one can speak of a look turned toward the face, for the look is knowledge, perception. I think rather that access to the face is straightaway ethical. You turn yourself toward the Other as toward an object when you see a nose, eyes, a forehead, a chin and can describe them. The best way of encountering the Other is not even to notice the color of his eyes! When one observes the color of the eyes one is not in social relationship with the Other ... The face is exposed, menaced, as if inviting us to an act of violence. At the same time the face is what forbids us to kill.

(Lévinas, 1985, pp. 85–86)

In this sense, the pedagogy of feeling, the culture of tenderness and caress, and the ethics of the fragility of the skin impose themselves as educational stations that can stem the conception of the other as an object for enjoyment, a need to be satisfied, a commodity to be enjoyed.

In short, we should make our bodies, every single body, no longer a simple place for performance, for productive frenzy, or for continuous efficiency. Rather, the body should be a place to listen to oneself and to others, a ground where we can meet others and ourselves, and a venue where we can host others and ourselves.

12 A Global Process of Psycho-Bodily Development

Mauro Magatti posits the concept of sustainability as the overall key to a possible redemption of the human condition from the claims of techno-finance and from humanity's sense of god-like omnipotence in its pursuit of unlimited growth and expansion. Magatti thus postulates sustainability in the human, as well as the environmental or social, sense, i.e., from a demographic, generational, and educational standpoint.

With reference to the aspect that most interests us here, Magatti (2017, p. 108) asserts:

> It can be said that school is one of the pillars of sustainability: without instruction and education, no discourse on future growth can be adequate. But it must be noted that school is no longer sufficient to sustain the speed of change; advanced societies need lifelong learning tools to prevent people from wasting their lives.

Education represents continuous training; it is a type of self-care but not in the sense of an individualistic and narcissistic process (as a form of egocentric withdrawal from the world). Instead, education expresses interest in the world; it is a form of relationship with the world itself because self-care must be rooted in relationships with others and should be characterized by mutual existential enrichment.[1]

Present-day needs demand extreme education and self-care, as is evident from the contemporary dissemination of eating and body

---

[1]   On the ethical and social value of self-care as a means to counter incorrect individualistic and solipsistic interpretations, see the fundamental Foucauldian analysis in *La cura di sé* (1996) and *L'ermeneutica del soggetto* (2003). See also Mortari (2009).

image disorders. Prevention, relationships, and education are connected to each other and vital for our reality.

The complexity of the contemporary hybridization of man and machine mentioned in other chapters of this book, the exasperated cult of the perfect body that is always publicly exhibited, and the obsession with food and its purity all correlate with the pervasive pathologies and mental illnesses of hypermodernity. These disorders are now viral in anthropological and social contexts that are marked by existential anxiety, continuous depressive drifts, and the exasperated need for efficiency and productivity (that are becoming less and less sustainable for human beings).

Conversely, the following holds true for human well-being.

> To better specify, in a positive way, what well-being is, it can be said that well-being, in which health is embodied, consists in the "right measure": temperance, proportion, convergence between the parts and the whole ... here we refer to exquisitely Greek concepts: Plato and the medicine of Hippocratic origin looked at the complexity, the somato-psychic totality of man.
>
> Well-being was configured precisely within this bio-psychic totality as symmetry, proportion, balance between forces.
>
> *(Clerici et al., 2010, p. 59)*

It is essential to attend to the profound meaning of education without taking an abused and sterile rhetorical stance. Thus, it is important to reflect intensively on ethical and existential aspects:

> All this in essence points to the fundamental rule – a very ancient one: do not do things in excess. It seems a very simple imperative, but following it is not at all simple: temperance, or the right measure, which is the highest message left to posterity by the Greek world, is extremely difficult to implement today. Modernity is in fact characterized by a basic ambivalence. It is as if the soul of today's man is split in two in the technological society: on one hand we are educated and encouraged to seek body perfection, modeling

> it with diets, gyms, even surgery, and on the other hand every kind
> of eating pleasure is offered, even junk food. In summary, there is
> a continuous oscillation between asceticism and hedonism. On the
> one hand obesity is rampant, on the other hand there is the
> spasmodic search for weight loss, sometimes carried out in an
> obsessive, fanatic, dangerous way for health.
>
> *(Clerici et al., 2010, pp. 106–107)*

In fact, education should ultimately be aimed at the inculcation of orientation, discernment, balance, strength, and the skills required for autonomous cognition.

Education can transmit all the virtues that people need to avoid becoming psychologically fragile, incapable of forming their own opinion, and manipulable by ideologies and the tyrannies of marketing. Those who do not develop the skills of autonomous orientation on the basis of their own values and reasoning can often become victims of others, subject to the directives of other individuals, or subordinate to the rules dictated by marketing.

Being educated denotes overcoming the laziness we encounter when we are not forming our own ideas. This lethargy is symbolic of the difficulty of reasoning, which represents the fear that characterizes every personal choice that does not receive external approval. Education must also focus on themes pertaining to the physics of bodies, encounters between human bodies, recognition of our own corporeality, and identification of the materiality of others.[2]

> Once again the Greek concept of "right measure" re-emerges, today
> more relevant than ever. The wisdom of the ancients shows us the
> way to eliminate many sufferings induced by the artificial
> conditions of our daily life ...

---

[2] In this sense, we speak about the recognition of the psychic dimension of others through our own body. Orienting ourselves in an enteropathic sense means comparing the dimensions, postures, and gestures of our body with those of others. This educational skill enables the awareness of our corporal dimension through the physical dimensions of others. For further details, see De Monticelli (1998).

> To prevent the authentic suffering caused by the two opposing forms of excess, obesity and anorexia, from growing in new generations, it is essential to recalibrate the Greek exhortation on the "right measure" in respect of the experiences of our young people.
>
> *(Clerici et al., 2010, pp. 195–196)*

The body dimension is also very significant because human growth is in many aspects related to the body. For instance, our emotions and their progressions, gestures, feelings, and postures all change during human development (Gamelli, 2012). As Frati (2012, p. 114) notes: "The subjective psychological dimension is built up within a global process of psycho-bodily development, where the bodily dimension is inextricably linked to our encounter with the world, our sensations and our thoughts." According to Foucault (1978), self-awareness enhances the ability to resist a power exercised on our bodies (control that is today exerted by marketing and social dynamics that dictate how we must be and behave).

For Nietzsche, education is the appreciation of beauty. Beauty does not inhabit frenzy and speed; instead, it can be found in aesthetic contemplation, mystery, and the secrets harbored in every person. In Nietzsche's view, beauty can be found through a prolonged meditation on the world, lingering over phenomena and contemplating landscapes.[3] This outlook is very different from contemporary perspectives. Demetrius emphasized that education awakens individuals, allowing them to see beyond the apparent and transcend aspects that are commonly consolidated (i.e., in the contemporary sense, a person can surmount fashion trends and marketing laws and logics).[4] Such education helps people to courageously discover and

---

[3] In this regard, Nietzsche (1910, p. 156) employed the following metaphor: "The slow arrow of beauty. The noblest kind of beauty is that which does not transport us suddenly, which does not make stormy and intoxicating impressions (such a kind easily arouses disgust), but that which slowly filters into our minds, which we take away with us almost unnoticed, and which we encounter again in our dreams."

[4] For further details, see Demetrio (2009); and on this same theme, cf. also Gabrielli (2011).

disclose hidden points of view, privilege shadows over uniform light, and prefer the solitude of the conscious conscience over the accommodating and flattering noise of those who are lazy and do not develop a personal opinion or thought. This viewpoint promotes the capacity of sustaining the burden of living, making life an occasion for growth, and making it an opportunity for evolution while aware of the obstacles and difficulties that existence entails. Courage, patience, contemplation, consciousness, slowness (against the frantic time of our age), and profound, community-based feelings are necessary for all this to become possible.

> Operating in the direction of maximizing the psychological, psychophysical and psychosocial well-being of people cannot be the exclusive competence of psychologists, it must be a common goal of all those who in any way deal with individuals, groups, organizations and institutions, since (as 150 years of scientific psychology has now definitively underlined) every single human being is in continuous and intense relationship with everything that surrounds him, be it to be considered as "physical, material and environmental reality" or as "human relationship, social and relational reality," and only the harmonious insertion of each person in their physical and interpersonal environment (work, school, friendship, affective, etc.) can therefore allow the conditions necessary for a level of well-being that is minimally compatible with the overall health of people to be actually achieved.
>
> (Frati, 2012, p. 244)

In conclusion, it is also particularly necessary for humanity to reactivate the existential and powerful wonder without which our living becomes mere survival. Thus, Szymborska's deeply felt poem seems to symbolically seal the spirit of this book:

> Yesterday, I behaved badly in the cosmos.
> I spent all day without asking any questions,
> I did not let anything surprise me.

I carried out my daily activities, as an obligation.
Inspiration, exhalation, step by step,
duties, but not a thought that went beyond
leaving the house and returning home.

(Szymborska, 2006, p. 71)

References

Aceranti, A. , Gabrielli, F. , and Cocchi, M. (2013) *Genesi del crimine violento: Tra psichiatria, biologia, filosofia*, ed. A. De Filippo. Lugano: Ludes University Press.

Acquati, C., and Saita, E. (2017) *Affrontare insieme la malattia: Il coping diadico fra teoria e pratica*. Milan: Carocci.

Adorno, T. W. (1974) *Minima moralia: Reflections from Damaged Life*. London: Verso.

Agamben, G. (2006a) *Che cos'è reale? La scomparsa di Majorana*. Vicenza: Neri Pozza.

Agamben, G. (2006b) *Che cos'è un dispositivo*. Milan: Nottetempo.

Amendola, A., Del Gaudio, V., and Tirino, M. (2017) Dell'orgia e della seduzione: Baudrillard come precursore del pensiero post-human. *Mediascapes Journal*, 9, 70–85.

American Psychiatric Association (2013) *Diagnostic and Statistical Manual of Mental Disorders*, 5th ed. (*DSM-V*). Milan: R. Cortina.

Anitha, L., Alhyssaini, A. A. , Alsuwedan, H. I., Alnefaie, H. F., Almubrek, R. A. , and Aldaweesh, S. A. (2019) Bulimia nervosa and body dissatisfaction in terms of self-perception of body image, in *Anorexia and Bulimia Nervosa*, ed. H. Himmerich and I. J. Lobera. London: Intechopen, pp. 23–33. DOI: http://dx .doi.org/10.5772/intechopen.84948.

Anzieu, D. (2017) *L'Io-pelle*, trans. it. Milan: R. Cortina.

Arnocky, S., Perilloux, C., Cloud, J. M., Bird, B. M., and Thomas, K. (2016). Envy mediates the link between social comparison and appearance enhancement in women. *Evolutionary Psychological Science'* 2, 2, 71–83.

Attia, E., Steinglass, J. E., Walsh, B. T., Wang, Y., Wu, P., and Schreyer, C. (2019) Olanzapine versus placebo in adult outpatients with anorexia nervosa: A randomized clinical trial. *The American Journal of Psychiatry*, 176, 449–456.

Aubert, N. (2003) *Le culte de l'urgence: La société malade du temps*. Paris: Flammarion.

Badiou, A. (2016) *Alla ricerca del reale perduto*, trans. it. Milan: Mimesis.

Baiardini, I., Abbà, S., Ballauri, M., Vuillermoz, G., and Braido, F. (2011) Alexithymia and chronic diseases: The state of the art. *Giornale italiano di medicina del lavoro ed ergonomia*, 33, 1 (SupplA), A47–52, 12.

Barthes, R. (1980) *La camera chiara*, trans. it. Turin: Einaudi.

Bateson, G. , Jackson, D. D. , Haley, J. , and Weakland, J. H. (1956) Toward a theory of schizophrenia. *Behavioral Science* 1, 4, 205–275.

Baudrillard, J. (2002) *Screened Out*. New York: Verso.

Bauman, Z. (2000) *La solitudine del cittadino globale*, trans. it. Milan: Feltrinelli.

Bauman, Z. (2005) *Work, Consumerism and the New Poor*. Maidenhead: Open University Press.

Bauman, Z. (2006) *Amore liquido, sulla fragilità dei legami affettivi*, trans. it. Bari: Laterza.

Bauman, Z. (2010) *Consumo, dunque sono*, trans. it. Rome and Bari: Laterza.

Beauchamp, P. (1985) *Uno e l'atro testamento: Saggio di lettura*, trans. it. Brescia: Paideia.

Benasayag, M. (2015) *Il cervello aumentato l'uomo diminuito*, trans. it. Trento: Erikson.

Benasayag, M. (2018) Psicoanalisi in progress nella era della digitalizzazione: Intervista con Miguel Benasayag. *Ricerca Psicoanalitica*, trans. it. Franco Angeli, 29, 1, 11–27.

Benasayag, M. (2019) *Funzionare o esistere?*, trans. it. Milan: Vita e Pensiero.

Benjamin, W. (2000) I "passaggi" di Parigi, in *Opere complete*, vol. XI, trans. it. Turin: Einaudi.

Besiner, J. M. (2013) *L'uomo semplificato*. Milan:Vita e Pensiero.

Besiner, J. M. (2010) *Demain les posthumains*. Paris: Puriel.

Binbay, T., Mısır, E., Onrat Özsoydan, E., Artuk, M., Fidan, S., Karakiraz, A., Önder, E., Öztürk, A., Sayin, M.B., Ulaş, H., Akdede, B., and Alptekin, K. (2017). Psychotic experiences in the adaptation process to a new social environment. *Turkish Journal of Psychiatry*, 28, 1, 1–10. DOI: 10.5080/u14975.

Bion, W. R. (1962a) *Una teoria del pensiero traduzione italiana in analisi degli schizofrenici e metodo psicoanalitico*, trans. it. Rome: Armando Editore.

Bion, W. R. (1962b) *Apprendere dall'esperienza*, trans. it. Rome: Armando Editore.

Bjornsson, A. S., Didie, E. R., Grant, J. E., Menard, W., Stalker, E., and Phillips, K. A. (2013) Age at onset and clinical correlates in body dysmorphic disorder. *Comprehensive Psychiatry*, 54, 7, 893–903. DOI: 10.1016/j.comppsych.2013.03.019.

Blond, A. (2008) Impacts of exposure to images of ideal bodies on male body dissatisfaction: A review. *Body Image*, 5, 3, 244–250. DOI: 10.1016/j.bodyim.2008.02.003.

Blowers, L. C., Loxton, N. J., Grady-Flesser, M., Occhipinti, S., and Dawe, S. (2003) The relationship between sociocultural pressure to be thin and body dissatisfaction in preadolescent girls. *Eating Behaviors*, 4, 3, 229–244.

Blythe, J., and Cedrola, E. (2013) *Fondamenti di marketing*. Milan and Turin: Pearson, Italia.

Bodei, R. (2019) *Dominio e sottomissione: Schiavi, animali, macchine, intelligenza artificiale*. Bologna: Il Mulino.

Bowlby, J. (1969) *Attachment and Loss*. New York: Basic Books. *Attaccamento e perdita*, vol. I, *L'attaccamento alla madre*, trans. it. Turin: Bollati Boringhieri, 1972.

Braidotti, R. (2017) *Per una politica affermativa: Itinerari etici*, trans. it. Milan and Udine: Mimesis.

Bratman, S. (1997) Health food junkies. *Yoga Journal* (September/October), 42–50.

Bratman, S., and Knight, D. (2000) *Health food junkies: Orthorexia nervosa – Overcoming the obsession with healthful eating*. New York: Broadway Books.

Bruckner, P. (2001) *L'euforia perpetua: Il dovere di essere felici*, trans. it. Milan: Garzanti.

Brunborg G. S., Andreas, J. B., and Kvaavik, E. (2017) Social media use and episodic heavy drinking among adolescents. *Psychological Reports*, 120, 3, 475–490.

Brytek-Matera, A. (2012) Orthorexia nervosa: An eating disorder, obsessive-compulsive disorder or disturbed eating habit? *Archives of Psychiatry and Psychotherapy*, 1, 55–60.

Besossi Jussi, E. (1993) Distanza originaria e relazione, in M. Buber, *Il Principio dialogico e altri saggi*, ed. A. Pomo, trans. it. Cinisello Balsamo: Edizioni San Paolo, p. 292.

Bude, H. (2014) *Gesselschaft der angst*. Hamburg: Hamburger Edition.

Calvino, I. (1986) *Sotto il sole giaguaro*. Milan: Garzanti.

Campa, R. (2015a) Il ruolo del potenziamento umano nelle guerre del future. *Futuri*, 6, 83-93.

Campa, R. (2015b) Biopolitica e biopotere: Da Foucault all'Italian Theory e oltre. *Orbis Idearum*, 2, 1, 125–170.

Carbone, M. (2016) *Filosofia-schermi: Dal cinema alla rivoluzione digitale*. Milan: R. Cortina.

Carr, N. (2011) *Internet ci rende stupidi? Come la rete sta cambiando il nostro cervello*, trans. it. Milan: R. Cortina.

Cavalli, G. (2017) *Crescere e far crescere, spunti teorici e applicativi per il lavoro relazionale*. Gessate: Sephirah Editore.

Chou, H. T., and Edge, N. (2012) "They are happier and having better lives than I am": the impact of using Facebook on perceptions of others' lives. *Cyberpsychology, Behavior and Social Networking*, 15, 2, 117–121.

Chugg, K., Barton, C., Antic, R., and Crockett, A. (2009) The impact of alexithymia on asthma patient management and communication with health care providers: A pilot study. *Journal of Asthma*, 46, 2, 126–129.

Clerici, F., Gabrielli, F., and Vanotti, A. (2010) *Il corpo in vetrina Cura, immagine, benessere, consumo tra scienza dell'alimentazione e filosofia*. Milan:Springer.

Cocchi, M., Gabrielli, F., Gerbino, A., and Tonello, L. (2016) *Di fronte alla vita: Antropologia dello stupore e biochimica dell'esistenza*. Palermo: Plumelia.

Contardi, R. (2005) *L'interpretazione dei sogni, libro del secolo: L'immagine tra soggetto e cultura*. Milan: Franco Angeli.

Curi, U. (2013) *Passione*. Milan: R. Cortina.

D'Agostino, J., and Dobke, M. (2017) A plastic surgeon's perspective on stereotyping and the perception of beauty, in *Perception of Beauty*, ed. Martha Peaslee Levine. London: IntechOpen, London. DOI: 10.5772/intechopen.69634. Available from: www.intechopen.com/chapters/56059.

Damasio, A. (1994) *Descartes' Error: Emotion, Reason, and the Human Brain*. New York: Putnam.

Damasio, A. (2003) *Looking for Spinoza: Joy, Sorrow, and the Feeling Brain*. New York: Harcourt.

D'Aurizio, C. (2018) Al di là della comunicazione e del controllo: Deleuze e la politica della creazione, *Segni e comprensione*, 32 n.s., 94, 168–183. DOI: 10.1285/i18285368aXXXIIn94p168.

Del Rey, A. (2018) *La tirannia della valutazione*, trans. it. Milan: Eleuthera.

Deleuze, G. (2000) *Poscritto sulle società di controllo*, in *Pourparler*, trans. it. S. Verdicchio. Macerata: Quodlibet, pp. 234–241.

Deleuze, G., and Guattari, F. (2002) *Che cos'è la filosofia?* trans. it. Turin: Einaudi.

Deleuze, G., and Guattari, F. (2010) *Mille piani: Capitalismo e schizofrenia*, trans. it. Rome: Castelvecchi.

De Monticelli, R. (1995) *L'ascesi filosofica: Studi sul temperament platonico*. Milan: Feltrinelli.

De Monticelli, R. (1998) *La conoscenza personale: Introduzione alla fenomenologia*. Milan: Guerini e Associati.

Demetrio, D. (2009) *L'educazione non è finite: Idee per difenderla*. Milan: R. Cortina.

De Pascalis, P. (2013) *Vigoressia: Quando il fitness diventa ossessione*. Rome: Il Pensiero Scientifico.

Derrida, J. (1996) *Donare il tempo: La moneta falsa*, trans. it. Milan: R. Cortina.

Derrida, J. (2007) *Toccare, Jean-Luc Nancy*, trans. it. Genoa:Marietti.

Dickinson, E. (2005) *The Poems of Emily Dickinson: Reading Edition*, ed. R. W. Franklin. Cambridge, MA, and London: Belknap Press of Harvard University Press.

Donini, L. M., Marsili, D., Graziani, M. P., Imbriale, and M., Cannella C. (2004) Orthorexia nervosa: A preliminary study with a proposal for a diagnosis and an attempt to measure the dimension of the phenomenon. *Eating and Weight Disorders*, 9, 2, 151–157.

Donini, L. M., Marsili, D., Graziani, M. P., Imbriale, M., and Cannella, C. (2005) Orthorexia nervosa: Validation of a diagnosis questionnaire. *Eating and Weight Disorders*, 10, 2, e28–e32.

Durbano, F. (2018) Unmet needs and future developments, in *Psychotic Disorders: An Update*. London: Intechopen. DOI: 10.5772/intechopen.7732.

Edelman, G., and Tononi, G. (2000) *Un universo di coscienza: Come la materia diventa immaginazione*. Turin: Einaudi.

Ehrenberg, A. (1999) *La Fatigue d'être soi*. Paris: Odile.

Ehrenberg, A. (2019) *La meccanica delle passioni: Cervello, comportamento, società*, trans. it. Turin: Einaudi.

Eposito, R. (2002) *Immunitas: Protezione e negazione della vita*. Turin: Einaudi.

Esquirol, J. M. (2018) *La resistenza intima: Saggio su una filosofia della prossimità*, trans. it. Milan: Vita e Pensiero.

Fallon, P., Katzman, M., and Wooley, S., eds. (1994). *Feminist Perspectives on Eating Disorders*. London: Guilford Press.

Fassino, S., Amianto, F., and Abbate-Daga, G. (2009) The dynamic relationship of parental personality traits with the personality and psychopathology traits of anorectic and bulimic daughters. *Comprehensive Psychiatry*, 50, 3, 232–239.

Feldman, J. M., Lehrer, P. M., and Hochron, S. M. (2002) The predictive value of the Toronto alexithymia Scale among patients with asthma. *Journal of Psychosomatic* Research, 53, 6, 1049–1052.

Ferrari, S. (1998) *La psicologia del ritratto nell'arte e nella letteratura*. Bari and Rome: Laterza.

Ferrari, F., and Nancy, J.-L. (2003) *La pelle delle immagini*, trans. it. Turin: Bollati Boringhieri, Turin.

Ferrari, E., and Ruberto, M. G. (2012) La bigoressia o dismorfofobia muscolare: Una nuova patologia emergente. *Bollettino della Società Medico Chirurgica di Pavia*, 125, 2, 373–377.

Fisher, J. (2017) Guarire la frammentazione del sé. Come integrare le parti di sé dissociate dal trauma psicologico. Milan: R. Cortina.

Floridi, L. (2017) *La quarta rivoluzione: Come l'infosfera sta trasformando il mondo*, trans. it. Milan: R. Cortina.

Fonagy P., and Moran, G. S. (1994) Psychoanalytic formulation and treatment: Chronic metabolic disturbance in insulin-dependent diabetes melitus, in *The Imaginative Body*, ed. A. Erskine and D. Judd. London: Whurr Publishers, pp. 60–86.

Fonagy, P. (1991) Thinking about thinking: Some clinical and theoretical considerations in the treatment of a borderline patient. *International Journal of Psycho-Analysis*, 72, 4, 639–656.

Foucault, M. (1978) *Microfisica del potere: Interventi politici*, trans. it. Turin: Einaudi.

Foucault, M. (1996) *La cura di sé*, trans. it. Milan: Feltrinelli.

Foucault, M. (2003) *L'ermeneutica del soggetto: Corso al Collège de France 1981– 1982*, trans. it. Milan: Feltrinelli.

Foucault, M. (2004) *La volontà di sapere: Storia della sessualità*, vol. I, trans. it. Milan: Feltrinelli.

Foucault, M. (1998) Il combattimento per la castità, in *Archivio Foucault: Interventi, colloqui interviste, 3, 1978–1985: Estetica dell'esistenza, etica, politica*, ed. A. Pandolfi, trans. it. Milan: Feltrinelli, pp. 172–184.

Franzini, E. (2018) *Moderno e postmoderno: Un bilancio*. Milan: R. Cortina.

Frati, F. (2012) *Il lato oscuro della mente: l'io di fronte ai cambiamenti*. Molfetta: Edizioni la Meridiana.

Fraze, J. L. (2000) Women's perspectives on the thin ideal in the development of eating disorders (Doctoral dissertation 2001, University of Georgia). Dissertation Abstracts International, 61, 8, 3073A–3073A.

Freedman, R. J. (1984). Reflections on beauty as it relates to health and adolescent females. *Women and Health*, 9, 29–45.

Freud, S. (1913) *Totem und Tabu: Einige Übereinstimmungen im Seelenleben der Wilden und der Neurotiker*. Leipzig: Hugo Heller.

Freud, S. (1923) *The Ego and the Id*. Standard ed., vol. XIX. London: Hogarth.

Fromm, E. (1991) *I Cosiddetti sani: La patologia della normalità*, trans. it. Milan: Arnoldo Mondadori.

Gabrielli, F. (2011) *L'incantesimo dello sguardo. Riflessioni antropologiche e proposte educative sui giovani*. Lugano: Ludes University Press.

Gabrielli, F. (2012) Philosophy and psychiatry: The violated body in the era of the invisible man, *NeuroQuantology*, 10, 2, 19–209.

Gabrielli, F., and Garlaschelli, E. (2016) *Estasi e frenesie dell'uomo contemporaneo: Brevi note sulla povertà dell'esperienza, tra filosofia e musica*. Lugano: Ludes University Press.

Gabrielli, F., and Garlaschelli, E. (2017). *Il paradigma fenomenologico-ermeneutico: Husserl, Heidegger, Gadamer, Lévinas, Ricoeur, Derrida.* Mantova: La Cittadella.

Gabrielli, F., and Garlaschelli, E. (2018) *Il debito fenomenologico: Un tracciato teoretico.* Milan: Glossa.

Gabrielli, F., Carta, A., and De Filippo, A., eds. (2016) *Percorsi di criminologia clinica.* Lugano: Ludes University Press.

Gabrielli, F., Garlaschelli, E., and Guarracino, V. (2017) *Antropologia della lacrima: Escursioni filosofiche e letterarie.* Bologna: Minerva.

Gabrielli, F., Grassi, P., and Le Breton, D. (2015) *Breve storia dell'adolescenza,* trans. it. Lugano: Ludes University Press.

Gabrielli, F., Carta, A., Fogliaro,P., and Scuotto, A. (2015) Violent food: Anthropology of eating disorders in the technical age. *New Medicine* 19, 2, 78–80. DOI: 10.5604/14270994.1169806.

Gabrielli, F., Cocchi, M., Tonello, L., Carta, A., De Filippo, A., Amore, M. D., Abielle,L., and Bozzi, A. (2014) The vulnerable woman: Anthropological contexts of violence, *Zeszyzty Naukowe Collegium Balticum,* 8, pp. 214–226.

Gadamer, H. G. (1988) *L'attualità del bello,* trans. it. Genoa: Marietti.

Gaddini, E. (1984) *Se e come sono cambiati i nostri pazienti fino ai nostri giorni.* Milan: R. Cortina.

Galimberti, U. (1983) *Il corpo.* Milan: Feltrinelli.

Gallagher, S. (2005) *How the Body Shapes the Mind.* Oxford: Oxford University Press.

Gallese, V. (2006) La molteplicità condivisa: Dai neuroni specchio all'intersoggettività, in A. Ballerini, F. Barale, S. Uccelli, and V. Gallese, *L'Umanità nascosta,* ed. S. Mistura. Turin: Einaudi, pp. 207–270.

Gamelli, I. (2012) *Sensibili al corpo: I gesti della formazione e della cura.* Milan: R. Cortina.

Garano, C., Dettori, M., and Barucca, M. (2016) Ortoressia e Vigoressia: Due nuove forme di fanatismo? *Cognitivismo Clinico,* 13, 1, 185–200.

Garner, D. M. (1991) *EDI-2 Eating Disorder Inventory 2: Professional Manual.* Odessa: Psychological Assessment Resources.

Glaeßner, G.-H. (2002) Sicherheit und Freiheit. *Aus Politik und Zeitgeschichte,* B 10(11), 3–13.

Green, A. (2011) Les cas limite: De la folie privée aux pulsions de destruction et de mort. *Revue Française de Psychanalyse,* 75, 2, 375–390.

Grion, L., ed. (2012) *La sfida postumanista: Colloqui sul significato della tecnica.* Bologna: Il Mulino.

Groesz, L. M., Levine, M. P., and Murnen, S. K. (2002) The effect of experimental presentation of thin media images on body satisfaction: A meta-analytic review. *International Journal of Eating Disorders*, 31, 1, 1–16.

Guanzini, I. (2017) *La tenerezza: La rivoluzione del potere gentile*. Milan: Ponte alle Grazie.

Han, Byung-Chul (2012) *La società della stanchezza*. Milan: Nottetempo.

Han, Byung-Chul (2015a) *Nello sciame: Visioni del digitale*, trans. it. Milan: Nottetempo.

Han, Byung-Chul (2015b) *The Burnout Society*. Stanford, CA: Stanford University Press.

Han, Byung-Chul (2015c) *The Transparency Society*. Stanford, CA: Stanford Briefs.

Han, Byung-Chul (2017a) *Il profumo del tempo: L'arte di indugiare sulle cose*, trans. it. Milan: Vita e Pensiero.

Han, Byung-Chul (2017b) *The Agony of Eros*. Cambridge, MA: MIT Press.

Han, Byung-Chul (2017c) *Saving Beauty*. Cambridge: Polity Press.

Han, Byung-Chul (2018) *The Expulsion of the Other: Society, Perception and Communication Today*. Cambridge: Polity Press.

Han, Byung-Chul (2019) *Eros in agonia*. Milan: Nottetempo.

Hanna, E., Ward, L. Monique, Seabrook, Rita C., Jerald, M., Reed, L., Giaccardi, S., and Lippman, Julia R. (2017) Contributions of social comparison and self-objectification in mediating associations between Facebook use and emergent adults' psychological well-being. *Cyberpsychology, Behavior and Social Networking*, 20, 3, 172–179.

Harrison, K. (2000) Television viewing, fat stereotyping, body shape standards, and eating disorder symptomatology in grade school children. *Communication Research*, 27, 5, 617–640.

Hausenblas, H. A., Janelle, C. M., Gardner, R. E., and Hagan, A. L. (2002) Effects of exposure to physique slides on the emotional responses of men and women. *Sex Roles*, 47, 11/12, 569–575.

Hay, P., Mitchison, D., Lopez Collado, A. E., González-Chica, D. A., Stocks, N., and Touyz, S. (2017). Burden and health-related quality of life of eating disorders, including avoidant/restrictive food intake disorder (ARFID) in the Australian population. *Journal of Eating Disorders*, 5, 1, 1–10.

Heidegger, M. (1988) *La Poesia di Hölderlin*, trans. it. Milan: Adelphi.

Heinberg, L. J., and Thompson, J. K. (1995) Body image and televised images of thinness and attractiveness: A controlled laboratory investigation. *Journal of Social and Clinical Psychology*, 14, 4, 325–338.

Hilbert, A., Petroff, D., Herpertz, S., Pietrowsky, R., Tuschen-Caffier, B., and Vocks, S. (2019). Meta-analysis of the efficacy of psychological and medical treatments for binge-eating disorder. *Journal of Consulting and Clinical Psychology'* 87, 91–105.

Hillman, J. (2001) Malinconia senza dei: Introduzione, in *Arcipelago malinconia: Scenari e parole dell'interiorità*, ed. B. Frabotta. Rome: Donzelli, pp. 3–16.

Hume, D. (1971) Trattato sulla natura umana, vol. I, Sulle passioni, vol. II, in *Opere*, trans. it. Bari: Laterza.

Irigaray, L. (2013) *Elogio del toccare*, trans. it. Genoa: il Melangolo.

Irtelli, F. (2016) *Illuminarsi di ben-essere*. Rome: Armando Editore.

Irtelli, F. (2018) *Contemporary Perspectives on Relational Wellness: Psychoanalysis and the Modern Family*. New York: Palgrave Macmillan.

Irtelli, F. (2019) *Rosso smeraldo : L'epoca delle psicosi bianche*. Rome: Armando Editore.

Irtelli, F., and Vincenti, E. (2017) Successful psychopaths: A contemporary phenomenon, in *Psychopathy: New Updates on an Old Phenomenon*, ed. F. Durbano. London: IntechOpen. DOI: 10.5772/intechopen.70731.

Isetta, G. (2015) Accident and plasticity: Thinking about aging philosophically in *Philosophical Exercises*, 10, 97–110.

Jaeggi, R. (2017) *Alienazione: Attualità di un problema filosofico e sociale*, trans. it. Rome: Castelvecchi.

Janet, P. (1929) *L'évolution psychologique de la personnalité*. Paris: Chahine.

Jankélévitch, V. (1998) *La musica e l'ineffabile*, trans. it. Milan: Bompiani. Einaudi.

Kaës, R. (1996b) *La parola e il legame: processi associativi nei gruppi*, trans. it. Rome: Borla.

Kaës, R. (1999) Il gruppo e il lavoro del preconscio in un mondo in crisi. *Koinos*, 1, 38–61. Originally publ. in French, 1996.

Kaës, R. (2012) *Malessere*. Rome: Borla Editore.

Kaës, R. (2014) Di quali risorse dispone la psicoanalisi di fronte al malessere contemporaneo. *Atti del Seminario di Studi Internazionali. Università degli Studi di Napoli "Federico II."*

Kanayama, G., and Pope, H. G., Jr. (2011) Gods, men, and muscle dysmorphia. *Harvard Review of Psychiatry*, 19, 2, 95–98.

Kant, I. (1798) *Antropologia dal punto di vista pragmatico*, trans. it. Milan: Einaudi, 2010.

Kim, J., and Lennon, S. J. (2007) Mass media and self-esteem, body image, and eating disorder tendencies. *Clothing and Textiles Research Journal*, 25, 1, 3–23.

Koven, N. S., and Abry, A. W. (2015) The clinical basis of orthorexia nervosa: emerging perspectives. *Neuropsychiatric Disease and Treatment*, 11, 385–394.

Krebs, G., Quinn, R., and Jassi, A. (2019) Is perfectionism a risk factor for adolescent body dysmorphic symptoms? Evidence for a prospective association. *Journal of Obsessive-Compulsive and Related Disorders*, 22, 100445. DOI: 10.1016/j.jocrd.2019.100445.

Lacan, J. (2006) Il *seminario, Libro II, L'io nella teoria di Freud e nella tecnica della psicoanalisi* 1954–1955, trans. it. Turin: Einaudi.

Lasch, C. (1985) *L'io minimo: La mentalità della sopravvivenza in un'epoca di turbamenti*, trans. it. Milan: Feltrinelli.

Lazzarini, A. (2011) *Polis in fabula: Metamorfosi della città contemporanea*. Palermo: Sellerio.

Le Breton, D. (2007) *Il sapore del mondo: Un'antropologia dei sensi*, trans. it. Milan: R. Cortina.

Levinás, E (1985) *Ethics and Infinity: Conversations with Philippe Nemo*, trans. Richard A. Cohen, Pittsburgh, PA: Duquesne University Press.

Levinás, E. (1989) Time and the other, in *The Levinas Reader: Emmanuel Levinas*, ed. Seán Hand. Oxford: Blackwell, 1989.

Levinás, E. (2003). *Totality and Infinity: An Essay on Exteriority* [1961], trans. A. Lingis. Pittsburgh, PA: Duquesne University Press.

Levinás, E. (2005). *Il tempo e l'altro*, trans. it. Genoa: Il Nuovo Melangolo.

Levinás, E. (2008) *Etica e infinito: Dialoghi con Philippe Nemo*, trans. it. Troina: Città Aperta.

Lipovetsky, G. (1995). *L'era del vuoto: Saggi sull'individualismo contemporaneo*. Milan: Luni.

Lipovetsky, G. (2003). *L'Ere du vide: Essai sur l'individualisme contemporain [1983] [The Era of Emptiness: An Essay on Contemporary Individualism]*. Paris: Gallimard.

Lipovetsky, G. (2019) *Piacere e colpire: La società della seduzione*, trans. it. Milan: R. Cortina.

Longo, G. O. (2003) *Il simbionte: Prove di umanità futura*. Rome: Meltemi.

Lorenzi, P., and Pazzagli, A. (2006) *Le psicosi bianche*. Milan: Franco Angeli.

Louw, D. J. (2017) Aesthetics of the naked human body: From pornography (sexualised lust object) to iconography (aesthetics of human nobility and wisdom) in an anthropology of physical beauty, in *Perception of Beauty*, ed. Martha Peaslee Levine. London: IntechOpen.

Lovelock, J. (2019) *Novacene: The Coming Age of Hyperintelligence*. London: Penguin Books.

Luhmann, N. (1979) Note lessicali, in *Potere e complessità sociale*, trans. it. Milan: Il Saggiatore.

Lumley, M. A., Neely, L. C., and Burger, A. J. (2007) The assessment of alexithymia in medical settings: Implications for understanding and treating health problems. *Journal of Personality Assessment*, 89, 3, 230–246.

Magatti, M., (2017) *Cambio di paradigma: Uscire dalla crisi pensando il future*. Milan: Feltrinelli.

Maffesoli, M. (2003) *L'istante eterno: Ritorno del tragico nel postmoderno*, trans. it. Rome: Sossella.

Mahler, M. S., Pine, F., and Bergman, A. (1975) *The Psychological Birth of the Human Infant: Symbiosis and Individuation*. New York: Basic Books.

Malabou, C. (2000) *Plasticité*. Paris: Léo Scheer.

Malabou, C. (2005) *The Future of Hegel: Plasticity, Temporality and Dialectic*, trans. Lisabeth During. London and New York: Routledge.

Malabou, C. (2009) *Ontologie de l'accident: Essai sur la plasticité destructrice*. Paris: Léo Scheer.

Marion, J. L. (1987) *Dio senza essere*, trans. it. Milan: Jaca Book.

Martin, M. C., and Kennedy, P. F. (1993) Advertising and social comparison: consequences for female preadolescents and adolescents. *Psychology and Marketing*, 10, 6, 513–530.

Mathieu, J. (2005) What is orthorexia? *Journal of the American Dietetic Association*, 105, 10, 1510–1512.

Mazzeo, R. (2015) Preface, in M. Benasayag, *Il cervello aumentato, l'uomo diminuito*. Trento: Erikson.

Merleau-Ponty, M. (1972) *Fenomenologia della percezione*, trans. it. Milan:Il Saggiatore.

Merlini, F. (2019) *L'estetica triste: Soluzioni e ipocrisia dell'innovazione*. Turin: Bollati Boringhieri.

Merini, A. (1997) *Titano amori intorno*. Milan:Edizioni La Vita Felice.

Merzenich, M. (2013) *Soft-Wired: How the New Science of Brain Plasticity Can Change Your Life*. San Francisco, CA: Parnassus Publishing.

Miller, N. E., and Dollard, J. (1941) *Apprendimento sociale e imitazione*. New Haven, CT: Yale University Press.

Mills, J. S., Shannon, A., and Hogue, J. (2017) Beauty, body image, and the media, in *Perception of Beauty*, ed. Martha Peaslee Levine. London: IntechOpen.

Mills, J. S., Polivy, J., Herman, C. P., and Tiggemann, M. (2002) Effects of exposure to thin media images: evidence of self-enhancement among restrained eaters. *Personality and Social Psychology Bulletin*, 28, 12, 1687–1699.

Minkowski, E. (2004) *Il tempo vissuto: Fenomenologia e psicopatologia*, trans. it. Turin: Einaudi.

Molinari, E., and Castelnuovo, G., eds. (2012) *Clinica psicologica dell'obesità, esperienze cliniche e di ricerca*. Milan: Springer.

Möllmann, A., Dietel, F. A., Hunger, A., and Buhlmann, U. (2017) Prevalence of body dysmorphic disorder and associated features in German adolescents: A self-report survey. *Psychiatry Research*, 254, 263–267.

Mongardini, C., ed. (2009) *L'epoca della contingenza: Tra vita quotidiana e scenari globali*. Milan: Franco Angeli.

Mordacci, R. (2017) *La condizione neomoderna*. Turin: Einaudi.

Morin, E. (2000) *La testa ben fatta: Riforma dell'insegnamento e riforma del pensiero*, trans. it. Milan: R. Cortina.

Mortari, L. (2009) *Aver cura di sé*. Milan: R. Cortina.

Mulders-Jones, B., Mitchison, D., Girosi, F., and Hay, P. (2017). Socioeconomic correlates of eating disorder symptoms in an Australian population-based sample. *PLoS One*, 12, 1, e0170603. DOI:10.1371/journal.pone.0170603.

Nadkarni, A., and Hofmann, S. G. (2012) Why do people use Facebook? *Personality and Individual Differences*, 52, 243–249.

Nancy, J.-L. (1998) *Hegel: L'inquietudine del negativo*, trans. it. Naples: Cronopio.

Nancy, J.-L. (2002) Un pensiero finito, trans. it. Milan: Marcos y Marcos.

Nancy, J.-L. (2008) *Indizi sul corpo*, trans. it. Turin: Ananke.

Nancy, J. L. (2009) *Indizi sul corpo*, ed. M. Vozza. Turin: Ananke.

Nancy, J.-L. (2013) *Prendere la parola*, trans. it. Bergamo: Moretti & Vitali.

Natoli, S. (1997) *Dizionario dei vizi e delle virtu*. Milan: Feltrinelli.

Natoli, S. (2010) *Il buon uso del mondo: Agire nell'età del rischio*. Milan: Mondadori.

Nietzsche, F. (1964) Aurora, in *Opere di Friedrich Nietzsche*, ed. G. Colli and M. Montinari, vol. V, book 1, trans. it. Milan: Adelphi.

Nietzsche, F. (1910) *Human, All Too Human:A Book for Free Spirits*, trans. Helen Zimmern. Part I, Division Four: Concerning the Soul of Artists and Authors – Aphorism #149. London: Foulis, 1910.

Nietzsche, F. (1965) *Frammenti postumi 1876–1878*, trans. it., in *Opere di Friedrich Nietzsche*, ed. G. Colli and M. Montinari, vol. IV, book 2. Milan: Adelphi.

Niola, M. (2015) *Homo dieteticus*. Bologna: Il Mulino.

Østergaard, S. D. (2017) Taking Facebook at face value: Why the use of social media may cause mental disorder. *Acta psychiatrica scandinavica*, 136, 5, 439–440. DOI: 10.1111/acps.12819.

Pacilli, M.-G. (2014) *Quando le persone diventano cose: Corpo e genere uniche dimensioni di umanità*. Bologna: Il Mulino.

Palazzani, L. (2015) *Il potenziamento umano: Tecnoscienza, etica e diritto*. Turin: Giappichelli Editore.

Palvarini, P. (2013) *Anoressia e bulimia: Quali emozioni? L'approccio dinamico esperienziale*. Francavilla al Mare: Edizioni Psiconline.

Parisi, F. (2019) *La tecnologia che siamo*. Turin: Codice Edizioni.

Perniola, M. (1994) *Il sex-appeal dell'inorganico*. Turin: Einaudi.

Perucchietti, E. (2019) *Cyberuomo: Dall'intelligenza artificiale all'ibrido uomo-macchina. L'alba del transumanesimo e il tramonto dell'umanità*. Bologna: Arianna Editrice.

Pessina, A. (2015) Human enhancement: Il soggetto e la liberazione dalla normalità, *Rivista di Filosofia Neo-Scolastica*, 1–2, 449–454.

Petrosino, S. (2012) *Lo stupor*. Novara:Interlinea.

Petrosino, S. (2013) *Elogio dell'uomo economico*. Milan: Vita e Pensiero.

Petrosino, S. (2015) *L'idolo: Teoria di una tentazione: Dalla Bibbia a Lacan*. Milan: Mimesis.

Petrosino, S. (2019) *Il desiderio: Non siamo figli delle stelle*. Milan: Vita e Pensiero.

Phillips, K., and Hollander, E. (1996) Body dysmorphic disorder, in *DSM-IV Sourcebook*, vol. II, ed. T. A. Widiger, A. J. Frances. , H. A. Pincus, R. Ross, M. B. First, and W. W. Davis. Washington, DC: American Psychiatric Association, pp. 949–960.

Piaget, J. (1937) *La naissance de l'intelligence chez l'enfant*. Neuchatel, Paris: Delachaux and Niestlé.

Pirandello, L. (1960) L'umorismo, in *Saggi e scritti vari*. Milan: Mondadori.

Plotinus (2018) *The Six Enneadi: Plotinus*, trans. S. Mackenna and B. S. Page. Global Grey ebooks.

Pope, H. G., Jr. (2011) Media hype, diagnostic fad or genuine disorder? Professionals' opinions about night eating syndrome, orthorexia, muscle dysmorphia, and emetophobia. *The Journal of Treatment and Prevention*, 19, 2, 145–155.

Pope, H. G., Phillips, K. A., and Olivardia, R. (2000) *The Adonis Complex: The Secret Crisis of Male Body Obsession*. New York: Free Press.

Pope, C. G., Pope, H. G., Menard, W., Fay, C., Olivardia, R., and Phillips, K. A. (2005) Clinical features of muscle dysmorphia among males with body dysmorphic disorder. *Body Image*, 2, 4, 395–400.

Prensky, M. (2013). *La mente aumentata: Dai nativi digitali alla saggezza digitale*. Trento: Erickson.

Puhl, R., and Brownell, K. D. (2001) Bias, discrimination, and obesity. *Obesity Research*, 9, 12, 788–805.

Pulcini, E. (2001) *L'individuo senza passioni: Individualismo moderno e perdita del legame sociale*. Turin: Bollati Boringhieri.

Quintarelli, S. (2019) *Capitalismo immateriale: Le tecnologie digitali e il nuovo conflitto sociale*. Turin: Bollati Boringhieri.

Recalcati, M. (2017) *Contro il sacrificio. Al di là del fantasma sacrificale*. Milan: R. Cortina.

Recalcati M. (2019) *Le nuove melanconie: Destini del desiderio nel tempo ipermoderno*. Milan: R. Cortina.

Riva, M. (2012) *Legami deliranti: Psicopatologia e politica*. Milan: Mimesis.

Riva, F. (2015) *Filosofia del cibo*. Rome: Catelvecchi.

Roheling, M. V. (1999). Weight-based discrimination in employment: psychological and legal aspects. *Personnel Psychology*, 52, 4, 969–1016.

Rosa, H. (2005) *Beschleunigung: Die Veränderung der Zeitstrukturen der Moderne*. Frankfurt a. M.: Suhrkamp.

Rossi Monti, M. (2008) Psicopatologia e figure del presente (*Il Presente*, ed. P. F. Pieri), *ATQUE*, 3–4, n.s.

Rudd, N. A., and Lennon, S. J. (2001) Body image: Linking aesthetics and social psychology of appearance. *Clothing and Textiles Research Journal*, 19, 3, 120–133.

Roudinesco, E. (2000) *Perchè la psicoanalisi?* Rome: Editori Riuniti.

Rümelin, J. N., and Widenfeld, N. (2019) *Umanesimo digitale: Un'etica per l'epoca dell'intelligenza artificiale*, trans. it. Milan: Franco Angeli.

Sanavio, E., and Cornoldi, C. (2001) *Psicologia clinica*. Bologna:Il Mulino.

Sander, L. W. (2007) *Sistemi viventi*. Milan: R. Cortina.

Sartre, J.-P. (1956) *Being and Nothingness*, trans. H. Barnes. New York: Philosophical Library.

Savulescu, J., and Bostrom, N., eds. (2008) *Human Enhancement*. Oxford: Oxford University Press.

Schilder, P. (1973) *Immagine di sé e schema corporeo*. Milan: Franco Angeli.

Scardovi, G. (2017) L'ibridazione eccentrica: Alla ricerca di una libertà postumana, *Limiti e confini del postumano, Lo Sguardo – Rivista di Filosofia*, 24, 2, 203–225.

Scheler, M. (1979) *Pudore e sentimento del pudore*, trans. it. Naples: Guida.

Schmitt, C. (1999) *Il nomos della terra*, trans. it. Milan: Adelphi.

Schwartz, H. (1986) *Never Satisfied: A Cultural History of Diets, Fantasies and Fat*. New York: Doubleday.

Scoppola, L. (2007) Corpo e psiche: gruppalità e integrazione nella relazione di cura, in *L'intervento psicologico in oncologia: Dai modelli di riferimento alla relazione con il paziente*, ed. M. Cianfarini. Rome: Carocci Faber.

Selz, M. (2005) *Il pudore: Luogo di libertà*, trans. it. Turin: Einaudi.

Sennett, R. (1999) *L'uomo flessibile: Le conseguenze del nuovo capitalismo sulla vita personale*, trans. it. Milan: Feltrinelli.

Severino, E. (1986) *La filosofia dai Greci al nostro tempo: La filosofia contemporanea*. Milan: Rizzoli.

Shakespeare, W. (1623) *Macbeth*, in *Comedies, Histories, and Tragedies*. London: Isaac Jaggard and Edward Blount.

Shakya, H. B., and Christakis, N. A. (2017) Association of Facebook use with compromised well-being: A longitudinal study. *American Journal of Epidemiology*, 185, 3, 203–211.

Sidani, J. E., Shensa, A., Hoffman, B., Hanmer, J., and Primack, B. A. (2016) The association between social media use and eating concerns among US young adults. *Journal of the Academy of Nutrition and Dietetics*, 116, 9, 1465–1472.

Siegel, D. J. (2013) *La mente relazionale: Neurobiologia dell'esperienza interpersonale*, trans. it. Milan: R. Cortina.

Silesio, A. (1989) *Il pellegrino cherubico*, trans. it. San Paolo: Cinisello Balsamo.

Simmel, G. (2011) *Le metropoli e la vita dello spirito*, trans. it. Rome: Armando.

Simondon, G. (2011) *L'individuazione alla luce delle nozioni di forma e d'informazione*. trans. it. Milan: Mimesis.

Simmel, G. (2006) *Estetica e sociologia: Lo stile della vita moderna*. Rome: Armando.

Silvestri, M. (2015) La dissociazione delle origini. Freud e Janet: Un confronto doloroso, un dialogo pensabile. *Ricerca Psicoanalitica*, fascicolo 1, 101–123.

Solano, L. (2013) *Tra mente e corpo: Come si costruisce la salute*. Milan: R. Cortina.

Spitz, R. (1958) *Le première annèe de la vie de l'enfant*. Paris: Puf, trans. it. *Il primo anno di vita*. Armando, Rome: Armando, 1973.

Stice, E., and Shaw, H. E. (1994) Adverse effects of the media portrayed thin-ideal on women and linkages to bulimic symptomatology. *Journal of Social and Clinical Psychology*, 13, 3, 288–308.

Stice, E., and Whitenton, K. (2002) Risk factors for body dissatisfaction in adolescent girls: a longitudinal investigation. *Developmental Psychology*, 38, 5, 669–678.

Stirone, V. (2018) Focus: E pur si muove! Psicoanalisi, mondo e contemporaneità. *Ricerca Psicoanalitica*, 29, 1, 9–10.

Suciu, B. and Crişan, C. (2020). Feeding and eating disorders, in *Mental Disorders*. London: Intechopen. DOI: 10.5772/intechopen.92218.

Sutter, L. de. (2018) *Narcocapitalismo: La Vita nell'era dell'anestesia*, trans. it. Verona: Ombre Corte.

Szymborska, W. (2006) *Due punti*, trans. it. Milan: Adelphi.

Tagliapietra, A. (2009) *Il dono del filosofo: Sul gesto originario della filosofia*. Turin: Einaudi.

Terrinoni, E. (2019) *Oltre abita il silenzio*. Milan: Il Saggiatore.

Thompson, J. K., and Stice, E. (2001) Thin-ideal internalization: mounting evidence for a new risk factor for body image disturbance and eating pathology. *Current Directions in Psychological Science*, 10, 5, 181–183.

Tolksdorf, U. (1976) Strukturalistische Nahrungsforschung/Tolksdorf Versuch eines generellen Ansatzes. *Etimologica Europea*, 9, 64–85.

Tromholt, M. (2016) The Facebook experiment: Quitting Facebook leads to higher levels of well-being. *Cyberpsychology, Behavior and Social Networking*, 19, 11, 661–666.

Tsiropulos, K. E. (1999) *Sulla tenerezza*, trans. it. Sotto il Monte-Bergamo: Servitium.

Turnaturi, G. (2012) *Vergogna: Metamorfosi di un'emozione*. Milan: Feltrinelli.

Udo, T., and Grilo, C. M. (2018). Prevalence and correlates of DSM-5–defined eating disorders in a nationally representative sample of US adults. *Biological Psychiatry'* 84, 345–354.

Unterrassner, L. (2018). Subtypes of psychotic-like experiences and their significance for mental health. In F. Irtelli. *Psychosis: Biopsychosocial and Relational Perspectives*. London: IntechOpen, DOI: 10.5772/intechopen.78691. Available from: www.intechopen.com/chapters/62216.

Vannini, M. (2003) *La morte dell'anima: Dalla mistica alla psicologia*. Florence: Le Lettere.

Velotti, S. (2017) *Dialettica del controllo: Limiti della sorveglianza e pratiche artistiche*. Rome: Castelvecchi.

Vincenti, E. (2017) Letture, illuminarsi di ben-essere. *Ricerca Psicoanalitica*, 28, 1, 118–120.

Vincenti, E., and Irtelli, F. (2018) *Familiar-mente: Legami e prospettive che non-ti aspetti*. Rome: Armando Editore.

Wolfe, A. (2014) Weekend confidential: Ray Kurzweil looks into the future. *Wall Street Journal*, May 30.

Zamperini, A. (2007) *L'indifferenza: Conformismo del sentire e dissenso emozionale*. Turin: Einaudi.

Zambrano, M. (2003) *Note di un metodo*, trans. it. Naples: Filema.

Zizek, S. (2005) *Credere*. Rome: Meltemi.

Zizek, S. (2009). *Leggendo Lacan*, trans. it. Turin: Bollati Boringhieri.

Index

For EU product safety concerns, contact us at Calle de José Abascal, 56–1°,
28003 Madrid, Spain or eugpsr@cambridge.org.